UNLOCKING CREATIVITY

UNLOCKING
CREATIVITY

A PRODUCER'S GUIDE TO MAKING MUSIC AND ART

MICHAEL BEINHORN

HAL LEONARD BOOKS

AN IMPRINT OF HAL LEONARD CORPORATION

Published in 2015 by Hal Leonard Books
An Imprint of Hal Leonard Corporation
7777 West Bluemound Road
Milwaukee, WI 53213

Trade Book Division Editorial Offices
33 Plymouth St., Montclair, NJ 07042

Book design by Lynn Bergesen, UB Communications

Library of Congress Cataloging-in-Publication Data

Beinhorn, Michael.
 Unlocking creativity : a producer's guide to making music and art / Michael Beinhorn.
    pages cm
 ISBN 978-1-4803-5513-2 (pbk.)
1. Popular music--Production and direction. 2. Sound recording industry. 3. Creation (Literary, artistic, etc.) I. Title.
 ML3470.B444 2015
 781.1'7--dc23
                              2015015001

www.halleonardbooks.com

To my wife, Jordan, and my daughter, Mia,
who constantly inspire me with their love
and intense determination

CONTENTS

INTRODUCTION

For over a third of a century, I've been producing records in one form or another. During that time, I've worked on several records that were extremely successful. I created a tape-recording format, and I was nominated for a few Grammy Awards. Whatever I've worked on, I have always been utterly captivated by the magic that goes into, and is generated by, the creative process.

I'd like to think all this has given me unique insight into record production—even a degree of expertise. In spite of this, I seem to learn something new or encounter something I've never seen before on every project. This is because I try to be open to the creative process and its outcome without trying to dictate exactly how it has to go. I find if I simply show up to work and devote myself to it, everything falls into place.

This constant process of learning and being mindful of the artistic experience that record producing can be assures that my perspectives on what I do will never stop evolving, I'll never grow bored, and I'll never know everything there is to know about what I do. This is exactly how I want it. If I could no longer experience record producing in this way, it would cease to have meaning for me and I'd have to stop doing it.

You see, once upon a time, record production actually did lose its meaning for me. Once upon a time, I seduced myself into believing that I was a businessman—not an artist—and I began to envision producing solely as a means to make money. Once upon a time, the magic of doing this work faded away—along with the creative process—turning it into a tedious, chaotic, unrewarding waste of time and effort.

As this metamorphosis was taking place, I gradually lost sight of what had made record production incredibly satisfying, and even financially rewarding. The truth is, I was only good as a record producer when I viewed it as an artistic process. It only worked for me when I treated it as a form of my own personal expression.

This is the main reason I wanted to write this book—to bring to light exactly what this process is and how to use it wisely and creatively as it pertains to record production. The process starts with knowing exactly who you are in relation to your work. In my case, I discovered I'm not a businessman. I'm not an entrepreneur. I'm an artist. That's all I ever really wanted to be in the first place.

When I chose to be mindful of this, I found my way back to doing really good work as a producer. And when that happened, I felt a renewed sense of purpose. I wanted to share my experiences—not only what I've learned over many years of being a record producer, but also what I've seen since I became mindful of who I am and how I fit into the process of record making. Finally, I wanted to share my journey of starting out as an artist, attaining success, losing my way, then finally, returning to where I started. As a result of this journey, I've experienced some completely oppositional perspectives on life and have a heightened appreciation for all of them.

I feel that sharing this information is far more valuable than writing about which microphone preamps I used for recording the drums on the Soundgarden record *Superunknown*. There are more than enough books in the world that address the technical part of making a record, but none about a producer's intent when he makes a record. You can read dozens of articles and books that feature a hundred different people talking about which microphones they used when they recorded record X or how they set their stereo bus compressor, but you will almost never hear them address what prompted them to make these choices. You will never hear them speak about the intent—the need to express an emotion or a feeling—that motivates their decisions. Without someone addressing this aspect of record making, there will always be a disconnect and always the nagging question, "That sounds so good—but why did they do it?" This is another reason why I wrote this book.

In reading accounts of how masters have made records, I have found that few of them talk about the intent behind their choices, their methodology, the emotions they were trying to evoke, or their credo. On the surface, it seems like their choices were made without feeling or consideration for the music they were producing and were mainly about technique. This implies that those who wish to learn this art can act similarly. The world looks chaotic and meaningless to one who seeks knowledge from masters who don't provide deeper explanations for their actions or insight into their creative process. My goal is to expose the creative motivation and intent that influences the choices great producers make when producing great records.

Just as important, we need to recognize that there is tremendous need for an ethical and holistic approach to record production and artist development. This need has only grown over recent years due to the path that the people who run the so-called music business continue down. Let me put this into context for you.

Anything extraordinary about the music business was, is, and always will be based on the creative output of artists. This creative output has virtually nothing directly to do with managers, record company executives, or record companies. At best, they provide an environment that allows artists to create. At worst, they can completely undermine an artist's ability to create. The best thing any record company executive ever did was to recognize the seed of greatness within an artist and nurture it to fruition. The best thing any record company ever did was to bankroll an artist's truly creative process of fancy and offer them up to the world when they were ready for perusal.

Without the infrastructure these peripheral individuals provide, there'd be no business to sell music. However, without artists there'd be no need for infrastructure because there'd be no music to sell. Ideally, in the past, the artist served his muse and, like the patrons of yore, the record company either served the artist or maintained a symbiosis with him.

Sadly, throughout the past twenty to thirty years, instead of nurturing artists, the music business has excelled at marginalizing and trivializing its product while attempting to tailor it to appeal to as broad an audience as possible. When lucre became elevated to such a lofty height by the music business, the performers and artists followed suit. Instead of making art to make a living, the sole emphasis was suddenly on making money for its own sake, by any means necessary. In the process, the role of the artist/performer was replaced by that of the entertainer/entrepreneur.

Over centuries, music has evolved and finally, has been utterly commoditized. It is now a lifestyle choice, an appendage—the equivalent of a piece of clothing, a bottle of perfume, a pair of headphones—except that you still have to pay for those items.

And this point is infused with even greater irony when you consider that many of those other commodities are exactly what modern entertainers put their names onto when they make their long-awaited trade up from performer to entrepreneur.

In such a climate, is it any wonder that artists are extremely challenged to committing emotionally to what they create? It often feels as though many contemporary popular artists have no idea how to connect emotionally with, or through, their medium. This goes a long way toward explaining why there seems to be so little real feeling in much contemporary popular music—only the simulation of feeling. As a consequence, there is little or no real communication in the music between artist and listener—only the simulation of communication.

At the very essence of music is communication. Relieve music of its ability to speak to another human being, and it becomes an empty shell. It becomes the signifier for a message with no purpose or meaning.

The creation of music is somewhat reactive; it's based on the need to communicate an experience you have either within or outside of yourself. Apart from being highly expressive and highly communicative, it is also kinetic. It relies on the component of believability and engages in direct dialogue with an audience, unlike painting or writing. And for music to naturally communicate kinetically, we must find a path back to helping a creative artist commit emotionally to her own work, to help her truly invest in her creative process, and to outline an ethical and holistic approach to record making. This is what we'll explore in this book.

In a sense, the expression found in popular music is very similar to that in acting. Actors are considered great based on their ability to express themselves or to be believable in their craft. They often learn an acting method, a system by which they can become more pure and honest in self-expression.

The actor, playwright, and poet Antonin Artaud referred to actors as "athletes of the emotions." Considering the effect that composers such as Mozart and Beethoven had on the audiences of their day (and for so many years hence), isn't it logical to view them similarly? And haven't artists such as the Beatles also wielded extraordinary power over their audiences? What is a popular music vocalist if he is not an "athlete of the emotions," who must often compress the full emotional impact of his expression into a statement of less than four minutes?

I feel that in all people there is a bridge that connects the conscious mind, the unconscious, and the physical body. This bridge is where the act of being creative becomes a sensory experience and is at the core of all artists, whether they are actors, musicians, painters, or work in other media. This is where artists find their intent, sensitivity, expression, and motivation. The spontaneous act of creating and performing music is accompanied by an undeniable sensory experience within the artist that is directly related and proportional to the sensory experience that a listener has when he "feels" the music he is listening to.

If you allow the possibility that popular music is a unique and essential art form, with no less validity than any other, isn't it logical that the essence of this art form and its experience should be recognized, lionized, illuminated, shared, and even taught to those who wish (providing they have the innate talent) to learn it? If we can figure out methods to teach actors how to emote and be expressive, why can't we do the same for popular musical artists? Perhaps the question really ought to be, why doesn't anyone ever take this into consideration when they "develop" artists?

This goes back to some of the elements that make the work I do so much fun. These are the collaborative aspect, the communal effort, a group of people working together with one purpose in mind and no other agenda. Few thrills are greater than participating in a project where an artist surpasses her own expectations. From where I stand, this is one of the best and only ways to move forward and make great art. It is the only way I can imagine to make popular music that once again matters to people everywhere. Because, more than anything, people who hear music also want to feel it.

That's one more thing this book is about—not simply my perspective on making records, not just the credo or intent that drives my creative process, not just interesting ways to effect change in creative situations and the creative processes of others. It's also about what the creative process feels like when I am (or you are) in the midst of it. The fact is, everyone who creates has some kind of physical, somatic connection to their creative process—just the same as the audience who experiences the end result of that process does. Most people are simply not aware of it. When you're in touch with this sensory connection, you will always know what you're doing.

And, whatever you're going to do next.

1

THE RECORD PRODUCER

What is a record producer? Even though the job title seems to carry a lot of weight and has an almost heroic, mythical resonance to it, most people don't really know what a record producer does. In fact, most artists and record company executives don't even understand what record producers do, although many of them believe that simply having a specific producer's name on their recording will guarantee them success, even if the producer in question winds up contributing next to nothing.

On the surface, record production is comparable to a wide variety of jobs—from office manager to school teacher to film director to lion tamer (and, perhaps, clinical psychologist). Beneath the surface, a record producer is often an objective outsider, an independent consultant, a music fan, a song cowriter, an arranger, a recording technician, a computer programmer, an artist development specialist, a support system, a psychologist, and a catalyst. But at its core, record production is mainly about being a conduit that helps the entire creative process flow most efficiently while maximizing the creativity of all the participants on the project.

To be clear, a record producer's primary directive is to help the artist excel. The producer does this by illuminating the artist's creative path, demonstrating various ways the artist can reach the highest level of expressive ability, and often motivating or pushing the artist to reach this summit. Working with a record producer is ideally not only an enlightening experience for an artist but also character building and life changing. After working with a talented producer, the artist may never view his work the same way as before. He should feel as though he's leaving the project as a different person from when it began, with a brand-new perspective and skill set.

Each record producer has his own approach and methodology—there is no right, wrong, or even generally accepted way to produce a record. This is also what creates so much confusion regarding the producer's actual function. Some record producers are very hands-on, involving themselves in every aspect of a production, from the recording budget to song arrangements to songwriting to working with the artist on her performance and the nuts and bolts of the recording itself. The scope of this producer's work is anything in the creative process that, by his estimation, requires assistance.

Some producers are mainly involved in the technical side of a recording and are either minimally involved in the musical or creative side, or not at all. Some producers cowrite the music for a recording with the artist (and often perform on these recordings) but don't get very involved in how the actual recordings are made. In some cases, these producers are also songwriters who are eager to acquire a larger equity share of a recording by writing songs for their artists, and then producing them. Some producers do multiple projects simultaneously; they hire engineers to run their sessions for them and check in periodically but generally don't go to the studio to do hands-on work with the artists while the recording is underway.

The old-school record producer stereotype was an omniscient, evil genius—a pale-skinned, puppet master Svengali who intimidated and manipulated his bewitched charges while rolling with the jet set in the evenings and on weekends. The stereotypical new-school record producer is a clichéd, youngish, scruffy hipster in white kicks who gets all his clothes from multiple endorsement deals with apparel companies that outfit prominent sports figures. He wrote the book *How to Schmooze for Dummies*, is marketing his own "personal scent," has his own scale-model action figure (by Mattel), knows more about his iPhone than a microphone, drives a Mercedes S600 and a tricked-out white Range Rover, has two young, hot PA's who were exotic dancers in a former incarnation, and rolls with the jet set in the evenings and on weekends.

The bottom line is that record production is like any other form of work. It's time-consuming and requires dedication, skill, and a lot of effort.

Although there are many types of record producers, I tend to put them in one of two categories. In the first category is the producer who makes an artist's recordings sound like every other recording in the same genre. He has a sound that he is known for, and no matter what artist he works with he follows his very specific template and never deviates from it—not even for an instant. This approach tends to deliver the same, very quantifiable results every time it's employed.

In the second category is the producer who makes recordings in accordance with the way he hears things. This approach is more abstract, more personalized, caters to the uniqueness of the artist, and, consequently, is more open-ended. It can't deliver quantifiable results the way the other approach can, but you can pretty much guarantee that the end product will always be more personal and more interesting.

A record producer also functions as an objective third party, providing experience and expertise as an invaluable resource for an artist to draw from. The flip side of working with a producer is that she might either be personally uninvolved and detached from the projects she works on, or become proprietary and develop a sense of ownership regarding the artist's work. The former situation often occurs because the producer wants to get a job done quickly and be able to move on to her next job. The latter situation often occurs as a result of the record producer's ego. The title "record producer" establishes a specific hierarchy, and being the leader of a project can be very seductive for some people. These individuals often buy into the idea of what being a record producer looks like to others, and then take it too far.

I feel that to do this work properly, it's essential to contribute to it artistically. It's imperative to speak up when you have an idea that will improve or potentially save an artist's song and to stick to your guns if you believe in your idea. It's also vitally important to know when to disengage emotionally, to stop being an artist in your own right, and to let go of your great ideas if they are operating at cross-purposes with those of the artist or the project.

In the most ideal sense, a record producer should have no interest or agenda in dominating or manipulating what the artist does—just in intensifying and distilling it. As a fellow artist, he may see his function as being a conduit or a receiver that funnels ideas to the artist for the benefit of the creative process.

Therefore, it is essential to constantly exercise flexibility for the sake of the artist, the project, your own creative process, and your peace of mind. This occasionally requires giving up your preconceptions and your proprietary feelings, and somehow remaining as completely committed to the work as when you began. Being flexible may be the single most difficult—and important—aspect of producing records.

THE PRODUCTION PROCESS BEFORE RECORDING

Although some of the most important decisions on a recording project are made during its earliest days, this part of the process is often the least addressed, possibly because it's not very glamorous and involves a lot of intense work. The next few chapters address the ways I approach various stages of pre-production of a project before the actual recording starts. I tend to deal with the process in stages, because a methodical approach often encourages creative ideas to develop organically, instead of feeling forced.

Later on in the book, I'll provide more specific and in-depth explanations for how this all works.

Stage 1: Introduction/Interview. This stage entails meeting the artist, preferably via e-mail, and then meeting in person or over Skype, FaceTime, etcetera. This helps set the tone for how the artist and I will work together.

Stage 2: Flyover of Artist's Work. I listen to the artist's demos and previous recordings, watch his videos, assess his work, and get inside it. During this stage, I generally get a feel for who the artist really is as opposed to who he claims to be and what the artist is actually doing as opposed to what the artist imagines doing or wants to do. Combined with stage 1, this stage helps me determine whether working with this artist will be a good fit.

Stage 3: Creative Visualization. Assuming that the artist is an ideal candidate and there is a good rapport between us, specific groundwork is laid for the creative collaborative process to commence. During this stage, I complete my conceptual overview of who the artist is (as an individual), what the artist is (as a creative entity—whether she is a dedicated artist, an inspired dilettante, a skilled artisan, an unskilled enthusiast, or an exotic blend of these elements), and what the sum total of the recording may look like at completion. At this point, I start to develop a mental picture of the artist's future work (as it may be affected by our collaboration) and to envision the best ways to actualize and enhance the artist's maximum capabilities.

This visualization creates an understanding regarding how to move forward and will guide nearly every decision I make with regard to the artist and his project.

Stage 4: Preliminary Pre-Production. The artist and I commence our creative collaboration. Gradually, as this process deepens, I gain the artist's trust, an even deeper insight into the artist (musically and otherwise), and the artist's songs come more clearly into focus.

I refer to this stage as preliminary pre-production, and the technical aspect of it covers everything from examining and fixing song structures and song arrangements to band orchestrations, addressing performance issues, and so on. This stage could conceivably last for a couple of months and requires regular interactions between the artist and myself. Most of the interaction is via e-mail, Skype, or FaceTime, with one or two physical meetings per week (each of which might ideally last two to four hours). All of this will vary in accordance with the artist's needs, my recommendations, and other factors, such as how far away the artist lives from me.

There is also an interpersonal component to this stage. Working more closely with the artist, I now begin to experience him. All along, I've been intuitively "reading" the artist through his music. Now, being in closer proximity with him, I start "reading" him and begin connecting the creator to his creations. This also helps me develop an awareness of the artist's unique way of communicating ideas and feelings. I start to pick up on the artist's sensitivities and am mindful of them when communicating any ideas, critiques, or thoughts to the artist.

Among other things, I feel that my job is to create a safe environment for the artist, within which he feels comfortable and is aware that any concerns he has (creative or otherwise) will be heard and addressed. It's important that I'm always conscious of this if I'm going to win the artist's trust, help build his confidence and to provide him with the proper tools to navigate his creative journey. In doing this, I wind up developing an empathetic rapport with the artist, which helps me get an instinctive sense of what he truly requires.

Stage 5: Pre-Production. Once the artist's music is arranged and roughly orchestrated, other musicians can be brought into the creative collaboration process.

This is the pre-production phase of the project. Pre-production ideally lasts for two to three weeks (although, it can last even longer) and involves daily rehearsals. I'm present with the band throughout the process, with the possible exception of when specific band members need to rehearse together and focus on aspects of their performance.

At this point, all the musicians should know the music they will be recording intimately. They will already have been playing the songs together or heard the songs in demo form and learned them. They are prepared to work on aspects of performance as well as developing their parts further.

At this stage, I often record band performances while in rehearsal just to get a point of reference (or, on the odd chance that someone plays something great and subsequently, forgets it). I generally use a smartphone or a handheld digital recorder with built-in microphones. Taking these performance recordings out of rehearsal, I can listen forensically, make changes where applicable, and then go back in with band to implement them.

Stage 6: The Next Vista Awaits. The pre-production stage is completed. All of the songs we have been tirelessly working on are now ready to be recorded with, in some cases, new arrangements, and a fresh approach to performing them. The songs have strong foundations and (with noteworthy exceptions, such as parts that can be composed later in the recording—for example, percussion, keyboards, background vocals, additional guitar overdubs, strings, and brass) all the vocal and instrument parts have been written. We are now ready to transition into the recording studio, meet other members of the creative team (such as the engineering and technical contingent), and begin the next phase of the process.

AND WHAT HAPPENS AFTER YOU'RE IN THE STUDIO?

You've done all the preliminary work, and brought the artist's songs and performances to a level that even you couldn't have predicted. You've selected an engineer who you feel is a perfect fit with the artist. The heavy lifting of pre-production is done, and the siren's call of the recording studio beckons you forth. Now it's time to let your imagination run wild and have fun.

But nothing is ever as it seems. On the first evening of recording, at the first stroke of eleven o'clock, out of nowhere, everything suddenly goes haywire.

The bassist has forgotten all his parts and flips out. The guitarist has punched the singer in the face and blood is everywhere.

Everyone is ignoring the engineer, who can't stem the mounting tide of mayhem. Discord reigns and all hell has broken loose.

What the hell just happened? You thought you had it all figured out. Everything was going so smoothly and you had already begun to ease into this next phase. Suddenly, without warning all your perfectly laid plans have gone up in a puff of smoke. For whatever reason, the recording feels hexed, as if it's all magically come undone in an instant.

What do you do now?

It would be too easy to curl up in a ball, stick your head in the sand, and ignore what's happening. But you know that great recordings can't get done when the prevailing atmosphere is nihilism. You know how you would feel if you were suddenly in the middle of a creative war zone, without a road map or anyone else to help pick up the pieces. And you're not the kind of person who bails on something just because it hit an unexpected bump in the road. So, you do what any clearheaded, responsible individual does. You roll up your sleeves and take charge.

Kind of calls to mind that scene in *The Godfather Part III* when Michael Corleone exclaims, "Just when I thought I was out, they pull me back in!"

The first thing to do is restore order. You probably won't be able to fix anything this late in the evening, so you calm everyone down and make a plan to regroup. The next day, you head down to the recording studio and regroup the troops. They're in pretty bad shape but you've seen worse. They may have all gotten overwhelmed by the first day of being in the studio.

Who knows? You do the necessary damage control and everything resumes, this time, with no hiccups.

Some producers will blithely tell an artist that they're more of a cheerleader than a hands-on producer. Still other producers will show up at the studio at their leisure and sit on the couch all day making business deals on their iPhones. But you don't operate like that, because experience has taught you to look further down the road. You know that not only will the artists you're producing have to bear the consequences of any careless choices you make, but that in the long run, you'll also have to live with them, too.

And from this point on, everything you do will simply be an extrapolation of what you've done during the early stages of the project. It just needs to get recorded.

Now that you're at that stage, you begin strategizing with the engineer about how the band will be recorded—such as which microphones and signal paths will be used, which performers will be playing when the initial recording takes place, and so on. You pay attention to the integrity of each portion of each signal chain, their nuances, how they interact and eventually come together to assist in creating an integrated band sound. You know the general characteristics of each microphone, each preamp, equalizer, and compressor that can be introduced into a signal chain, so you have a strong sense of how to paint an evocative picture using these audio devices. Having such a broad palette to choose from is like being a kid in a gigantic candy store.

You review song structures and all aspects of performance with the musicians and make sure they know exactly what they'll be playing. This is where all that preliminary and pre-production work you did comes in so handy.

While you're keeping an eye on all the technical stuff, you're also paying close attention to the general mood and how each individual is holding up. You know the way this works. Everyone, at some point in the recording process, needs some one-on-one coaching. You know when to be encouraging, when to push hard, and when to hang back, leaving them alone so they can figure things out on their own. You also want to pay close attention in case another fracas, like the one at the outset of the project, happens again. Of course, it doesn't.

When the recording commences, you morph into a minutia-obsessed, multitasking maniac. You're constantly attentive and acutely attuned to everything around you. You can hear the tiniest subtleties being picked up by each individual microphone. You can tell what each person is feeling and if they're concentrating on their work just by listening to how they're playing. That's part of what makes this work as much fun as it is challenging.

You select the best versions of each song, and if you were recording only drums and bass first, you begin to record all of the overdubs. More setups, more signal processing, more coaching. This is the juncture where art and interpersonal dynamics meet. It's your milieu.

Finally come the vocals. Generally, you try to break them up by stopping every few days and recording other instruments so as to give the singer a break and let his voice cool down. On this particular project, you've already lost a lot of time and there is no wiggle room—there are only a few days to cut the vocals. You just have to hope that the singer's voice stays fresh for the entire time and doesn't give out. This is a big deal. After all, the vocals just happen to be the most important component in the entire project. With grim determination, you grit your teeth and dig in.

Panic, chaos, and everything else imaginable, ensues. You've seen it all before. Working closely with the vocalist and helping him through the bumpy patches, the vocals get completed.

And somehow, in the process, everything else gets recorded, too.

Joy of joys—everyone who hears it, loves it. You love it, too. Why wouldn't you? You worked your butt off making it.

And then, it's time to mix the recording. You get to listen back to months of hard work that finally have come to fruition. You recall all the stages it went through to attain completion. You gaze lovingly like a proud parent at all its component parts splayed out over a mixing console—one last time before it's committed to stereo forever and ever.

Then, as quickly as the project began, it's over. And, just as you have on so many other projects you've finished, you look back and wonder how it all managed to work out. Was it magic, talent, or just blind luck?

You've dodged another bullet. Phew.

DIALOGUE IN THE STUDIO

I was working on a recording with M. N. and his band. When it came time to record his guitar, I felt that he was holding something back in his performances. I needed to address this with him, but it had to be done without affecting his confidence or our intention to record his best performances.

Michael: Okay, let's stop for a minute and talk about what's going on here.

M. N.: Okay. What do you mean?

Michael: Well, I'm hearing you play this song and I'm not really feeling *you* coming through. I'm not getting you—your personality. I feel like you're hiding yourself behind a wall; like you just want to get this whole thing over with and you don't want anyone to see you while you're doing it. It's like you don't want to connect with anyone who's going to be listening to what you're doing.

M. N.: You're getting that just from listening to me play?

Michael: Yes, I am. And we—you—want to make this powerful, believable, right? Your performance—I assume you want it to connect with people who hear it.

M. N.: Well, yeah.

Michael: Okay, well, it's not believable and it won't be if you're not investing yourself in it—if you're not present in the room with us. You know, people who listen to music don't hear the other instruments. They go straight to the vocal. Everything else, to the listener, is an afterthought, even subliminal. You know?

M. N.: I don't really think about that, but yeah. I guess so.

Michael: But, that said, the vocal can't be meaningful if everything that's supporting it isn't performed with conviction. And that's why everything we're doing—down to getting the instrument sounds to coexist—it all matters so much.

M. N.: I know what you mean. It's always so hard for me to come into a recording and just do what I'm told. To play what I'm expected to play and then get paid and leave. What you want me to do is so different. It's kind of foreign. I can keep trying.

Michael: Okay, but there's more. I don't want to hear you *try* anything. You have to be fearless and unafraid. Do you mind if I make an observation?

M. N.: Sure. Anything.

Michael: I can feel that you're hiding part of yourself away. There's a lot of rage in there that you don't want to let out because you don't think anyone is going to like it or you. You think people will think less of you for letting it off the chain. But while you hold on to the rage, it just festers and cripples you—it holds you back creatively. I'm showing you the opportunity to release it, all of it. It's safe here. No one is judging you. I'm just a listener—someone who loves music and wants to share the experience of your releasing this intense emotion you have stored up inside of you. That's the only thing that matters at this very moment.

M. N.: Whoa. You can see all of that? *[Pauses. Starts to cry.]*

Michael: Yes, and it's vital for you to use this experience as a means to release what's inside you now. Play with all the intensity you have. This is the best way to free yourself and start living and enjoying your gift. Be here, play this song, and put your entire being into it. You can stop hiding. You have it in you—you have great talent.

M. N.: This is frustrating and scary. I know it's in me, I'm just not sure...

Michael: Come on, man. No excuses. We're here to help you get through this. I want to feel what you're really feeling come through your performance. I want to feel your anger; I want to feel your joy. If you risk letting people see who you are, then the singer will also feel it and she'll be challenged to let people see her, too. It's all cumulative, all down the line. This isn't just about playing a song—it's about raw emotions, expression, and release. All those emotions are trapped inside you and they need to get out. This is the way to do it. It's about making a commitment to what you're doing and leaving something of yourself behind. That's you leaving your mark on this music. That's what you want, isn't it?

M. N.: Let's roll it again. I'm ready.

2

PREP WORK

It never fails to amaze me that many people who identify themselves as record producers commence work on recording projects without knowing anything about the songs or artists they're going to record. Yep, you read that right. There are people getting paid cash money to make records who start a recording without knowing a single note of the music they're going to be working on. It's as though they think that everything will just magically happen while they leisurely sit back, dispense a few sage platitudes, and let the Pro Tools guy fix what doesn't sound right.

Even more bizarre to me are those record producers who have actually listened to the music they'll be working on and have no ideas or thoughts about how to improve any of it. I can't help but wonder if this sort of cavalier attitude would be permissible in any other business or type of work. How would you feel about having a surgeon stand over you, scalpel in hand, and as the anesthesia starts to kick in, he ever so casually mentions that he has no idea what he's supposed to be doing for you?

The fact is, nothing great has ever come from anyone passively sitting back and making neither a conscious effort nor contribution to what they were supposed to be doing. Especially not when their agreement to work on a project also represents a commitment to giving it their very best efforts.

All recordings need some degree of prep work. This may be as simple as listening to the songs you'll be working on and getting to know them. Personally, I feel it means getting immersed in them to the point where they become part of my DNA. And yes, I'm aware that by saying this I'm admitting that I develop a personal relationship with, and thereby a proprietary attitude toward someone else's music. For better or worse, that is how I work when I'm wearing my record producer hat. As a result, I must constantly be aware of when I'm becoming too proprietary toward someone else's music.

The way I see it, an artist is coming to me for guidance and I've represented myself as being the man for the job. I might as well sit down and listen to what she does. It also won't hurt if I take note of what feels right and wrong to me about it. Since I have connected with it and decided to work on it, I can invest myself in cracking its code and help make it feel as right as possible.

If you can detect that something in a piece of music doesn't feel right to you, sit with it and try to develop a deeper understanding of what feels wrong. First, it helps to identify what exactly is making you feel uncomfortable. For example, is there an issue with the song structure? If so, is it in the melody, chord selection, or chord sequence? Is there an arrangement or orchestration issue or is there an issue in the performance? Next, consider a solution that might improve this issue and how you can best put it into effect. It is always helpful to establish a baseline standard for both good and bad elements. For example, by combining your feeling for the artist's body of work with your personal aesthetics, you can establish a baseline for what you consider to be the best and worst ideas she has presented. Once you have established a baseline standard of the artist's best work, you can use that as a general point of reference. From there, you can help the artist to maintain everything he does at that baseline or attempt to surpass it.

Concentration and focus are necessary to assess and prep an artist's songs, and you should be prepared to spend as much time as possible in order to do this effectively. If you can't or won't invest yourself in working with an artist's music at this level, you have no business trying to produce it.

This stage of work doesn't end once pre-production begins, or even when the project goes into a recording studio. Well into the recording process, I have constant flashes of inspiration regarding new instrument parts, arrangement and performance ideas, and other embellishments. By remaining completely open to inspiration, the creative well never runs dry. Often, ideas and parts bubble up from my unconscious while I'm listening to something else I'm currently working on. An idea may pop into my head when I'm doing something completely mundane and meditative, like washing dishes or driving. Frequently, ideas come at night when my brain doesn't want to shut off and needs an excuse to keep working. This always reminds me of how excited I was as a little boy to stay up late. It hasn't really changed.

After listening to a song a few times, I generally have the entire structure memorized and can listen to it at will, using my mind as a playback device. I'll often work on music this way, focusing on what doesn't feel right and imagining a fix, a new part, and/or sound. I'll assess whether the music is speaking clearly to me and delivering all its emotion. Whenever the emotional content is lacking, I instantly lose my connection to the music. The same thing happens if the artist isn't connected with his own performance.

I generally know something isn't right if I begin paying attention to other things in my immediate environment rather than the music I'm listening to. This awareness guides me toward the sounds and/or parts that are interfering with my connection or ability to hear the music and helps me find a way to address the issue. Once the issue is dealt with and the song flow is restored, the distractions tend to vanish and the song comes back into focus.

It is essential to have an active imagination for this approach to work. I feel that a lifetime of daydreaming has assisted me in developing my own imagination and enables me to let it off the chain as often as possible. So does meditation, listening to many different kinds of music, pretty much all stimulating experiences and exposure to other forms of expression. I can't overstress how vitally important it is for the imagination to be allowed to run wild and expand, instead of being shoved into a box and constantly forced to conform. Often, doing something creative without the expectation of an outcome can be far more rewarding than performing the same action with a specific end result in mind.

My imagination has created a very rich and active fantasy life for me. When you imbue your inner world with the awareness that anything is possible, the outside world begins to reorient itself accordingly. If anything is possible, then anything can be imagined and, thereby, created. Having this alternate perception running concomitantly with whatever the perceived concept of reality is has been extremely helpful when I have to shut out the world and commune with my unconscious.

People may insist that creativity is a conscious act, but the unconscious is truly a bottomless wellspring to mine for greatness.

THE INTERVIEW PROCESS

Prior to working with a producer, the artist should get to know the producer and the producer can begin evaluating the artist. This is where the relationship between the producer and the artist begins. This doesn't need to be a formal interview, but that's basically what it is.

I feel it's important for me to get to know the artist as an individual while also becoming familiar with his work and process. Taking time to find out about his life, his background, likes, dislikes, family, what influenced him to become an artist, what/who inspires him, and so on, helps me to understand him and relate to him as an individual. Knowing about the artist's background can provide deeper insights regarding what motivates and drives him and generally makes it easier to work effectively with him. This may sound a bit too involved, but we are forming the basis for a very intimate relationship, and the better I can serve this relationship, the better the creative process will likely be.

Before meeting, I will sometimes ask the artist to write a paragraph on why he wants to do creative work. This is another way to see how he feels about what he is doing and what compels him to do it. It also helps focus his intent, because through this exercise, he's essentially being asked to concentrate on identifying what it is, thereby, making him consciously aware of it. This part of the process is optional and I only do it if it feels appropriate.

The initial meeting process is ideally conversational—relaxed and informal—and generally doesn't feel like an interview. Here are a few questions I might ask an artist when we meet:

What exactly are you looking for by doing creative work? If you haven't considered this question before, how does it make you feel now?

Would you be satisfied working in a big corporation or serving drinks in a bar, or is creative work something you couldn't imagine not doing?

Do you seek success?

Do you seek fame?

How do you define success?

How do you define appreciation from others for the work that you do? Is appreciation from others absolutely necessary?

What would it feel like/look like if you were to attain what you are striving for?

How do you view yourself?

Can you find positivity in loss or rejection and work through them?

Can you transform the experience of loss or rejection into something that inspires you to achieve your goals?

Can you see yourself moving beyond your present boundaries in order to achieve things you can't imagine at this moment?

What is a formative experience in your life that taught you about loss, or about pain?

What is a formative experience in your life that taught you about success, or about happiness?

What is a formative experience in your life that demonstrated to you that you needed to do creative work?

Do you have any specific questions you want to ask me (the producer) about how I work, my feelings about your music, or how I feel about anything else?

Post conversation, I often write down my thoughts about the experience of meeting the artist and the feelings I got from it. I consider how I felt speaking with him—if the experience felt good or if there were any weird or uncomfortable moments while we spoke.

Reviewing and analyzing my feelings helps me decide whether or not the artist is a good candidate to work with. These feelings are often a very accurate barometer for predicting what our relationship will become in any future creative collaboration.

3

PRELIMINARY PRE-PRODUCTION

Preliminary pre-production is the phase of a project when the artist and I begin to develop our relationship and establish the foundation of our creative collaboration.

I think of preliminary pre-production as adding some extra reinforcement to the foundation of a building. Since a house can only be as sturdy as its foundation, it makes sense to ensure that the foundation (and the entire structure) is as sturdy and durable as possible. Similarly, if you want a recording project to have some kind of lasting value, you'll want to reinforce its foundation in every way you can. The better prepared you are during the earliest stages of a project, the easier it will be to reflect the full intent and meaning of its creators.

This is also the phase of a recording project when the artist and I start to work intently on the artist's songs, both as a team and separately (generally absent other band members who are not involved in the songwriting process. In the case of bands that create music together, this dynamic changes according to the degree of participation in the writing process. Aspects of songs—such as lyrics, melodies, and melodic motifs—are still addressed directly with the band members who are responsible for them).

Laying this type of groundwork has repeatedly proven to be absolutely invaluable as the project develops (and it requires a deep level of commitment to the artist's music).

PROCESS DURING PRELIMINARY PRE-PRODUCTION

Preliminary pre-production is a highly analytical-intuitive process that operates better the better prepared one is. I've found that this stage of a recording project is relatively easy if I follow specific guidelines that expedite the process and help me get deeper into it. The following illustrates some of the methodology I often employ.

GOALS TO BE ACHIEVED

1. Establish a basic understanding between the producer and artist about where the artist needs to go creatively.
2. Establish an understanding of the artist's true intent, what she is capable of, and what she does best.
3. Establish a benchmark regarding the artist's performance and songwriting.
4. Address song rewrites (when required) and explain to the artist why the rewrite is necessary.
5. Develop complete arrangements or rearrangements of all the artist's songs.
6. Develop basic orchestration of all the artist's songs.
7. Examine harmony and chord usages, and how they interact with vocal melodies in all songs.
8. Develop a general understanding regarding textures to be used in basic tracks (such as bass, drums, guitar).
9. Examine lyrics, melodies, and phrasing; identify weak points and strong points.
10. Explore the concept of "feel" as it relates to vocal phrasing and other relevant instruments.
11. Establish sensory reference points for or with the artist that they can begin to identify, refer to, and use as emotional

benchmarks. These benchmarks are "points of interest" in an artist's work and can be a feeling in the body or a strong memory that is used as an anchor to recall an emotional state. This can help bring an artist into a deeper relationship with her work.

12. Assemble all the artist's song demos—even those of songs she has no intention of recording. I never know if the artist has a diamond in the rough laying around or discarded, and I often can't rely on the artist to be objective about this.

CRITERIA AND QUESTIONS I POSE TO MYSELF WHEN LISTENING TO THE ARTIST'S MUSIC

I do some self-inquiry to get an indication of how I feel about the music I'm listening to (while also figuring out how to make it work better structurally).

Song Analysis

Does this song make me feel good? Does it make me feel bad or uncomfortable? Does it make me feel things I don't want to feel? Was this intentional? In any case, am I experiencing what the artist intended to express when I hear it?

Does this song make me care about it and about the artist?

What is this song about?

Am I interested in, or ambivalent about, what the artist is trying to say?

Does this song speak to me? Could it speak to anyone?

Does this song have an intentional subtext (represented in either the lyrics, the music, or both)?

Is the artist capable of reaching me on an emotional level? Was he able to with this song?

Is this song devoid of any meaning or emotional resonance?

Is this song more about creating a mood than about structure and development or storytelling? Is the text of the song completely abstract, but still evocative of something specific?

Song Structure

How is the song built? What does its structure consist of in terms of form and instrumentation?

Do I feel that the structural integrity of the song is solid, or shaky?

Does the song's structure help or hurt it? If the structure is a nonstandard one (for example, something other than the standard ABABCAB), is my feeling objective or subjective?

How are the song dynamics? Are they engaging to me, or do they feel flat?

Does the song lift (become more dramatic or intense) where I feel it should?

Does the song breathe (create space or lull) where I feel it should?

After more consideration, does the song structure work? Why, or why not?

If the song doesn't work structurally, how can it be fixed?

Here's Something to Always Keep in Mind

Has this ever happened to you? You're listening to a new song demo, it's bouncing or lilting along beautifully and so appropriately—it's pressing all your buttons and has your attention. You're cruising along, buying it, eating it up, when all of a sudden—BOOM—something happens and—presto!—just like that, the magic is gone. Without any warning, the song instantly went from sensational to suck, and now that you've had the sucky part of the experience, the initial part you liked doesn't even sound good anymore.

Whatever might have been good about any song can be completely obliterated in a split second by a single wrong turn or deviation in the structure. Where music is concerned, the now is all that matters. Now is when you are hearing it, now is when you find it exciting, now is when you are tired of it. Music is a communicative art form, and it generates an immediate visceral response or feedback within a listener.

For this reason, it is vitally important to keep the interest level of a song as consistently high as possible by all means available. It is also vitally important to ensure that the structural elements are impeccable and that the song transitions appropriately from one part to the next.

SONG ORCHESTRATION

When the song is played on multiple instruments, what kind of instrumentation is being used?

What style of music is the song performed in?

Is the present instrumentation appropriate for the song?

Is the rhythm section supporting the melodic aspect of the song? If not, how is it weak? Is this weakness specific and localized, or general?

If there are issues with the rhythm section, are they with the drumbeats being used, the interaction between bass and drums, or is there a general issue between all the rhythm instruments?

Is the bass weaving—supporting and coloring the song and its melodies, and creating melodic counterpoint? Or, is the bass static—only playing root notes and adding no coloration beyond the obvious? Which approach is best for the song?

Is the combination of instruments creating excitement, or are they just dull?

Are there any interesting polyrhythms occurring in the rhythm section, or is the rhythm section playing all the same beats, hits, and accents? In certain rhythmic patterns, when bass-guitar, bass drum, and guitar hits all occur simultaneously, this can bog down a song and cause it to drag. In certain cases (for example, when a song that is propelled by eighth notes, or where it is an actual rhythmic motif), this may not apply.

Are the transitions from section to section good? Are there adequate drum (or other instrument) fills or interesting passing chords to get from section to section? (Poor transitions will often flatten the dynamics of a song.) Will the song work better if the transitions are edgy and uncomfortable?

Do sections build well internally, or do they remain flat throughout? If they don't build, is that okay?

Do the instrument sounds on the original song demo (or the proposed instrument sounds) represent the song well (accurately) or poorly (inaccurately)? By changing or reorchestrating the original instrument choices, does this drastically change the intent of the song? Is this constructive, or is it detrimental to the song?

Does each section of the song consistently cycle through a three- or four-chord sequence, which occurs without deviating over the course of four complete cycles? If so, does it make sense to modify the sequence in some way (on one or more complete cycles, once the initial chord sequence has been established)? Can this potentially make the song more engaging?

Does the song become tedious or repetitive? If so, where?

Can alternate chords, melodic lines, drumbeats, or bass parts be used to keep the song engaging? If so, where? Are you ready to reorchestrate some instruments?

Was the tempo established similarly for this song? Has the tempo for this song been established at all? Does the present tempo make the vocals sit and flow well?

When they rehearse, does the band consistently play certain songs too fast? Too slow?

VOCALS

Does the vocal phrasing work with the vocal melodies? Does the vocal phrasing work with the rhythm section and other instruments? If not, where is the problem? Why doesn't it work?

Are there too many syllables in any of the lyrics that interfere with the timing or phrasing of the vocals?

Are any lyrics being stressed or emphasized in the vocal performance? If so, where? Does this work? If so, why?

Is the vocal phrasing stiff, or is it loose? When the vocalist sings, are the vocals presented in discrete blocks that start and stop predictably at the beginning and end of bar lines, or do they flow organically over the song and embellish it? Which approach is more appropriate for the song?

DIALOGUE REGARDING SONG MODIFICATION

I am talking with J. B., who is the vocalist and songwriter for his band. One of their demos featured an amazing part that came at the end of the song and sounded completely extraneous to what had preceded it. I decided to address this with J. B.

Michael: This song is really great.

J. B.: Thanks. I think it has a lot of potential, too.

Michael: Yes, it does. I did notice something kind of odd about it, though. You know the end of the song, right? The tag? There's that part that happens there and it goes on and on for over a minute and a half.

J. B.: Yes, I like that part a lot.

Michael: So do I—in fact, I think it's amazing.

J. B.: Really? You think so?

Michael: Yes. But I'm confused about one thing. What's that part doing at the end of a song as a tag or an afterthought? It sounds completely extraneous to the song it's in. What purpose is it serving there?

J. B.: I'm not really sure.

Michael: Honestly, that part is my favorite thing you guys have presented for your record. I love it. Let me ask you this: does this part have to be at the end of this song? What would you think of taking that part and creating a whole new song with it?

J. B.: Really? So you think that should be a whole song?

Michael: No, that's a part. You can write a new song around that part.

J. B.: So what part of the song is it? The verse?

Michael: No, that part is epic. My feeling is, it would work best as the chorus. If it makes sense to you, you can start working on it. Build some parts around it. I suggest you work out a verse and a bridge. I think it'll sound awesome.

J. B.: Wow. I wasn't expecting this. All right, let me get into it and see what happens. I like the challenge.

DIALOGUE REGARDING PRELIMINARY PRE-PRODUCTION

C. C. is the singer and primary songwriter for his band, and we're having a discussion about the material he has been writing. He's sent me all of the songs he's written so far for his record. We're speaking because he's at a creative impasse. It's time to brainstorm and help get him moving.

C. C.: So, I think I've got all the songs we need.

Michael: But you're not quite there yet.

C. C.: What do you mean?

Michael: You've got more in you than what you've sent me. We both know that. This record is a pivotal moment in your career and you need to go as far as you can with it. You have more in you—you just haven't gone as deep as you need to go. I know it's uncomfortable for you to get to your core, but it's necessary if you want to go all the way and make the strongest statement.

C. C.: Okay, maybe I'm stuck. So, what do you think I should do?

Michael: Well, what motivates you? What moves and inspires you? Why are you doing this? What's a good song to you?

C. C.: When I write a song, I'm thinking about our fans. I try to write songs that our fans will like.

Michael: Okay, consider that this might be your first mistake.

C. C.: How's that a mistake?

Michael: Well, how do you know what these fans of yours really want? Do you know them personally? Do you live inside their heads? That's impossible. But you're investing yourself in trying to create something that they'll appreciate, something that will make them continue to like you. And what that really means is creating something that sounds like something else they've already heard from you. So how is that helping anyone? You're not actually giving them something they want—it's something you think they want. You can't know what people really want. You definitely can't know what they like, even if they've told you exactly what that is. It's a waste of time. The only thing that matters is what you like. So, the question is, what do you like?

C. C.: I don't know. Everything. Nothing.

Michael: Okay, let's try this: What music inspires you? Whose songwriting do you consider to be an influence?

C. C.: I dunno. The Beatles. Cream.

Michael: Okay, then start by writing a song that sounds like the Beatles and Cream. You can do that, right?

C. C.: Yeah, but it's not going to sound like our band. If I write something that way, it'll sound like something for my solo project. We need to sound like us so that people know who they're listening to. Besides, what if it doesn't work? What if my band doesn't like it?

Michael: Check this out. You guys already are your band—you don't need to keep reestablishing your identity. You already have your sound; you've established it and evolved into it through years of hard work. Write the music you love. Don't try to please anyone else or think about who you're writing for. When you have written a great song, you can show it to your band. When you guys get together and play it, it's going to sound like you because you already have your sound, your approach. And because you've actually tried to write something that feels good to you instead of something you think will feel good to someone else, it will be really, really good. Does that make sense to you?

C. C.: Hmmm.

Michael: You can do this—you know it. Write something that you want to hear—that you enjoy. It'll surprise you. Forget about trying to please any of these people you don't know. The best way to give them what they really want is to give them something you really care about.

4

PRE-PRODUCTION

I f preliminary pre-production is about establishing and reinforcing the foundation of a recording project, the pre-production stage is like having a terrific insurance policy on the foundation (and subsequently, everything else the foundation is supporting). Put another way, pre-production significantly improves an artist's odds of having better-than-average results with the material he already knows is good. Both stages tend to augment each other.

Pre-production is the stage at which I start working with the full band on song structures, orchestration, and performance, and rehearse everything so that we can all get a rough idea of how the final product will sound. It also gives me a chance to observe the dynamics among the musicians so I can see how they interact, if there are problems between them, and what potential issues might arise down the road.

By this point, I'll have spent a good deal of time with the primary songwriter(s) throughout the preliminary pre-production phase, communicating ideas regarding song structure and overall direction, in person, by regular contact with the artist via e-mail, FaceTime or Skype.

This groundwork has provided me with in-depth knowledge of all the music that will be recorded and given me insight regarding what the songs need to work properly and represent the artist's vision adequately. I've also developed a good intuitive sense of who the artist is and how to maximize this awareness for our mutual benefit.

As I have become familiar with the artist's songs, I've also made extensive notes regarding song arrangements (some of which have already been implemented with the artist prior to pre-production) and instrumentation and orchestration. These notes will be the basis for the pre-production stage.

When studying demo recordings and band performances, I listen for consistencies and inconsistencies in how the band plays together and how the band is using instrumentation and song structure to either augment or impair each song. I also listen for other elements such as song dynamics.

I find that proper usage of drums and bass is an essential part of good, unimpeded song flow. For example, the placement of bass drum hits is often a vital support to vocal phrases. Bass drum hits can be used to emphasize, push, answer, or otherwise embellish vocal phrases. Inversely, poor placement of bass drum hits can interfere with a vocal phrase, often taking the listeners' attention away from the vocal and causing them instead to unconsciously focus on how uncomfortable this disparity is making them. The bass guitar is similarly supportive to the vocal and in some cases, can provide countermelodies that interact with the vocal, make the harmonic content of the song more interesting, as well as providing added movement and decoration.

Generally, I will initially work with the bass and drums in rehearsal before moving on to the full band. The reasoning behind this goes back to building the strongest possible foundation for the music. Because bass and drums are foundational instruments in a band, it is essential to ensure that they are creating the best possible foundation for everything else.

After the rhythm section dynamic has been established, it is ideal to introduce the vocals and at least one additional instrument that provides a harmonic reference as well as accompaniment for the vocals. At this point, the emphasis is mainly on the rhythm section; however, introducing the other instruments helps to broaden the context. Working this way, I can see how the rhythm section interacts with vocal melodies as well as harmonic elements, and can make further adjustments if necessary.

The entire band become active participants in the creative process, watching the development of their songs as they are deconstructed—and then reconstructed—often making suggestions regarding any musical problems that arise. And when the entire band begins to rehearse, the songs can finally be experienced in the context of a larger picture.

It is important to note that through all these phases, establishing context for everything and constantly redefining it is very important. At every stage, each discrete element can be viewed from multiple perspectives—almost like a three-dimensional sculpture, which can be looked at from multiple angles. Taking this approach in pre-production helps all the creative participants view their own work in many different ways—and through other people's eyes. It also gives each one of them the opportunity to see their work at varying stages of completion, to examine how what they are doing interacts in real time with what everyone else is doing and to be aware of the significance of what they are doing at every moment.

PROCESS DURING PRE-PRODUCTION

While trying to keep the general atmosphere loose and nonregimented is important, having some guidelines to follow makes the pre-production stage of a recording project easier. When done correctly, this process also creates numerous opportunities to provide impromptu growth for the artists so they can develop organically. Here is some of the methodology I employ at this phase of a recording.

Band Analysis

To be clear—usage of these criteria is not mandatory. Having worked with a variety of artists over the years, I have found it extremely helpful in expediting the various stages of record making if I am clear about everyone's respective roles in the creative process. For me, making these observations has become more of a reflex than something I do consciously.

Interpersonal Observations

1. Who are the dominant band members? Who is the most dominant?
2. Who are the submissive band members?
3. Who are the most capable band members? Who is the most talented?
4. Who are the least talented members?
5. Which band members are troublemakers and likely to stir up drama on the project? Are there any?
6. Which band members are the peacemakers who maintain balance on the project? Are there any?
7. Which band members are intimidated by the process and are preparing to fold?
8. Which band members are weak? Who is the weakest? Will they attempt to undermine the creative process because of their weakness, and if so, how?

9. If a band member is in a position to undermine the creative process, is he replaceable? If so, by whom, and is that replacement readily available? Does he need to be on deck immediately?

10. Are there jealousies or resentments between any band members? If so, what are they, why are they, and how do they manifest?

11. Are any of the band members self-destructive and possibly ready to drag the entire process down with them?

12. Are there any substance abuse issues in the band? If so, are they manageable, or unmanageable?

13. Is there any other excessive or potentially disruptive behavior in the band?

14. Are there any external issues that create interference in the band?

15. Do any individuals in the band allow their personal lives to create any kind of interference or disturbance in the work space?

Technical Observations

1. Can the drummer play without a click, or is one required?

2. Can the drummer play well? Can he or she play at all?

3. Do the tempos work for each song now that the entire band is playing them?

4. What instruments are being used by the artist or band for recording, what is the variety of amplification, and so on?

5. Are all the songs written? If not, what state are they in? What do they require to be finished?

6. Is each song in the right key? With some rare exceptions, my experience has been that songs generally don't sound or

work as well if they are transposed into a different key from the one they were written in. This is mainly because the key a song is written in is a defining aspect of its character. When a technical piece of a song's inner workings is modified, that character is often changed and the song has a completely different feeling to it. In spite of this, songs are often transposed to fit the range of the vocalist so that he or she can sing them with greater ease. Unless the vocalist's ability to perform is being completely compromised because he has to sing far out of his range, this is not always the best reason to change the key of a given song. In some cases, it actually sounds good to hear a singer strain to grab a note. It's important to note that this is not as much of an issue when the song is being sped up or slowed down in varispeed, because those increments are usually much smaller than half tones.

HOW TO TELL WHEN A BAND MEMBER IS PREPARING TO FOLD DURING A RECORDING PROJECT

Performance anxiety, red-light fever, whatever you want to call it . . . we've all seen people in a variety of creative environments fail in epic fashion (and the experience is even more profound when the person failing is you). To describe this situation, I use the term *fold*, from poker (which I do not play, as life is enough of a gamble already), because it feels appropriate under the circumstances. In my experience, it can be incredibly beneficial to recognize these potential signs in advance of someone folding, especially on a recording session where time is money and, these days, little of either is in great supply.

A band member may be ready to fold when:

1. He suddenly becomes unusually quiet, if he is normally talkative.
2. He suddenly becomes unusually talkative, if he normally doesn't speak much. In either case, he begins acting out of character.
3. He starts having fits of erratic, nervous behavior that call undue attention to himself.
4. He starts to have trouble recalling his parts—even if they are simple. Notice when this begins out of nowhere and becomes a consistent habit.
5. If he is using a notational system to record his parts (or a recording device to recall and memorize them), he either forgets to use it or he selectively employs his system to the extent that his notes are sketchy and they wind up being useless.
6. He plays songs he's supposed to know differently each time, even after he's been given detailed road maps or created his own.
7. He becomes reticent and occasionally hostile when these issues are brought up to him (or if his proficiency comes into question).
8. He starts apologizing profusely for his performance (and for a variety of other things).
9. He starts (resumes or continues) some form of substance abuse unbeknownst to anyone else on the project. At some stage in the process, this substance abuse becomes obvious.
10. He begins to drift away from the other people on the project, spending more time on his own. This becomes conspicuous especially if he is close with some of the other musicians.

11. He becomes more emotionally fragile and easily intimidated by things that appear relatively harmless.
12. He seems distant and distracted all the time.
13. He may have had a recent upheaval in his personal, emotional, or psychological life.
14. He occasionally seems terrified and/or disoriented.
15. He starts sweating a lot for no reason.
16. He has an air of failure about him, is utterly lacking in confidence, and begins to make disparaging comments about himself.
17. His appetite fluctuates from day to day (mainly eating less).
18. He seems thoroughly dejected but actually appears relieved when he is told that he needs to be replaced.
19. It becomes apparent (or it comes to your attention) that he's abusing a substance.

Often, people who are in this state have a very distinct aura about them. It's best if they can be identified immediately (as specified in stage 5), taken aside, and coached through whatever issue they're dealing with. Occasionally, and only if absolutely necessary, there is no option but to replace them. If not addressed, their presence can affect the performance of other individuals in the creative space.

5

WHO, AND WHAT, IS AN ARTIST?

The term *artist* is used often and gratuitously these days when describing virtually any performer. However, most people don't understand what an artist actually is. Dictionary definitions aside, this is highly subjective territory, so here are some of my own thoughts on the subject.

First and foremost, an artist is someone who uses whatever medium he or she feels most inclined toward to express him or herself completely and fully. An artist usually feels that her medium picked her, instead of the other way around.

Generally speaking, being an artist is not a job—it's a calling.

An artist is kind of an alchemist. He has an innate ability to convert the raw material of his emotional state into distilled expression that communicates his feelings accurately to other people through the specific medium of his choosing.

An artist may not be a virtuoso in her chosen medium, but she is the very best when she is pursuing one specific thing: her own authentic truth. She knows that by constantly seeking and assessing her truth, she will always be able to tap into her own unique mode of expression.

Her commitment to expression may lead down many paths. Her popularity may suffer, and the relationship with her audience may change as she pursues what feels best to her instead of pursuing what could more likely maintain her popularity. She does this because she knows it's a far worse fate to become stale by repeating herself than it is to do something new, even though it may alienate those who have come to expect something familiar from her.

The artist's function isn't simply to express himself in order to fill the world with the fruits of his labor; he also creates to show the rest of the world what being expressive looks and feels like. He does this so they may follow his lead and find their own unique form of self-expression. By design, he is a leader and a source of inspiration in every sense. (The Russian painter Vassily Kandinsky addresses this in his 1912 book *On the Spiritual in Art*. In this work, Kandinsky compares the spiritual existence of humanity to a great pyramid—the pinnacle of which the artist has mission to lead the rest of humanity to.)

These days, entertainers are confused with artists and artists are expected to be entertainers. However, there is a difference: Although an artist can also be an entertainer, an entertainer can't always be an artist. An entertainer must serve someone else, but an artist ultimately serves only his truth.

An entertainer gives people what they think they want. An artist gives people what they don't know they want, but what they ultimately need. This is because true, expressive art communicates the artist's state honestly and truthfully and nourishes the soul of the listener.

A true artist is driven by faith in his talent and his intuition. He works tirelessly to maintain his authentic voice at all times and is constantly challenged. He is even fearless enough to challenge himself, his beliefs, and his ethics when he feels they must be questioned or have become stale.

For an artist, good enough is never good and good can never be good enough. There is always a better performance, a better version of a song, a better song to be written and a more immaculate means to express himself. This is why he is constantly evolving and striving toward attaining that singular feeling which may elude him his entire life, or may be his partner in the great dance into perpetuity.

He is a believer, aware that martyrdom may await him at every turn, yet fearless because he trusts the beacon of his talent to light his way through the darkness. In this way, the true artist knows he is unlike other people and, ultimately, must walk this road alone.

SOME GENERAL QUESTIONS ABOUT THE ARTIST YOU'RE WORKING WITH

These questions are general, and the answer to each question is unique to each artist. They are simply observations—meant to be introspective and not judgmental.

These questions can work in tandem with the impressions you got from inquiring how the artist sees himself and his process. It is always interesting to consider the disparities between how a person sees himself, and how he is seen by others. It's also worth considering that observations made of others are often based on aspects of our own character that we recognize in them.

In Which of These Areas Is the Artist Lacking in Confidence?

- His abilities?
- His vision?
- His music?
- His performance?

Let's Go Deeper:
What Is the Artist Truly Made Of?

Remember when you first asked the artist about his goals? What's your feeling about that now? Was her original assessment accurate, or not?

Does the artist's self-image or goals match with who she truly is or what she's actually capable of?

How honest is the artist with herself about what she's doing? Is she deluding herself in any way?

Assuming that the artist is truly talented, is that talent worth developing and working with?

Does the artist have the drive to achieve her goals? Is she capable of making an effort to achieve these goals, or is she unwilling to do so? Does she possess the ability to achieve her goals, but also unrealistic expectations regarding how to do so? Does the artist have a hidden agenda that interferes with her stated need to achieve her specific goals?

What is her level of experience regarding basic essentials of her craft, such as performing, songwriting, and studio work? Does she seem capable of and open to a breakthrough that will take her further in her own artistic development?

Can you and the artist work well together? When you and the artist speak, is there an unspoken understanding between you, or is your communication strained, laborious, confusing, and/or unclear?

Does the artist communicate ideas accurately? Does the artist have difficulty explaining her ideas? Does she communicate what she feels, or does she conceal her feelings and, instead, communicate something she thinks other people want to hear?

Does the artist have her own code-speak? Does she use images or adjectives when she explains her ideas? If this is a band, is there an internal code language among the band members that, once you have decoded it, makes their internal communication comprehensible? Is the artist (or band) willing to allow the producer access to this code language in order to establish a dialogue, or do they intentionally keep outsiders from penetrating their world? It's important to note that being aware of this is not the same as judging it; it's just fascinating to observe how a band can often be like a club or a minisociety.

Does the artist welcome being observed or critiqued? Does she hide to avoid being criticized or being noticed? Does she feel the need to control how people see her (while she is creating, performing, and so on)?

Is the artist comfortable with her own body and its function as a sensory instrument, or is she afraid of it? Does the artist do any type of physical or body activity (sports, exercise, yoga, meditation, therapy, healing) to keep herself in touch with her body and what it tells her about her world?

Conversely, does the artist do any type of physical activity that is dangerous or life threatening? In her lifestyle choices, is the artist a risk taker, a thrill seeker, self-destructive, or someone who simply enjoys being active?

Does the artist embrace her emotions, or does she avoid and even disavow them? Is she conscious of using her emotions as well as her life experiences as grist for her creative mill?

Does the artist ever reach a point in her own process where she begins to worry, overthink, or otherwise switch her perception from an intuitive place to a cerebral place? Are there specific issues or situations that set this off?

Does the artist feel more comfortable working from a cerebral place or working from an emotional or intuitive place? Can the artist switch between these states at will?

If, for the sake of a deeper connection to her work, she is asked to move from a cerebral to an intuitive state of awareness, is the artist willing or able to, or does this bring up issues of fear? Is she willing to confront and work through this fear if she sees doing so will help her to attain a greater level of creative freedom and expression?

Does the artist follow a regimen to motivate herself (or does she do any type of work, creative or otherwise, for this purpose)? Is the artist disciplined in finding ways to motivate herself, or is she inconsistent and disorganized?

Is the artist capable of building her own creative platform without the help of others? Does the artist rely on other people to feed her creative ideas? Does she derive cues from others before she feels comfortable doing anything? Does she require chord structures to work from, or can she create an idea without any accompaniment? When she composes songs, which comes first—the lyrics, the melody, or accompaniment?

If the artist is insecure, how is this manifested? Does she turn this insecurity outward (attacking or lashing out at others physically, emotionally, or psychologically), or inward (self-effacing, self-loathing, self-destructive)?

Is the artist a courageous explorer, unafraid of plumbing the depths of her expression, or is she a self-pitying victim, terrified of her own shadow and the opinions of others regarding her work?

Does she seek to blame others for any failures or issues she may have? Does she consistently talk about situations in her past that she feels have damaged her, or about people who have slighted her in some way (even when her perception of being slighted may be completely imaginary or subjective)?

Does the artist create imaginary problems for herself and others? Does she blow relatively small issues out of proportion?

What is the artist's work ethic? Is she dedicated to working hard or does she slack off and look for ways to sabotage her workflow?

Does the artist create static around her so she can consciously or unconsciously divert work and responsibility away from her? Does she give her work highest priority, or does she relegate it to the periphery behind other issues that she invests with greater scrutiny or passion? Do these other issues create obstacles in the artist's creative life and keep her from moving forward in her creative work? Does she use these other issues as a means of escaping from her creative work, other people, her life, and/or herself?

Is there a constant air of confusion around the artist? Do people she works with (such as other artists and musicians) tend to have difficulty concentrating, remembering their parts, or maintaining their place in a given piece of music? Do they inexplicably start acting this way only when they are around the artist?

Does the artist surround herself with people or other musicians who irritate her and inadvertently create problems that she must always fix? Is she the alpha-leader in the band, delegating chores or responsibilities that her bandmates are incapable of performing, and then finishing what was left undone while complaining about their inefficiency? Does she spend an inordinate amount of time talking about these other people and the situations they've created that she has to fix?

Does it seem that she is actually conscious of this dynamic and might even enjoy it? Is it possible this dynamic makes her feel better about herself?

Does the artist crave stability, or does she revel in chaos?

Is the artist conscientious toward the other musicians she works with? If she prefers chaos, is she aware that this can be detrimental to her coworkers and to their joint efforts? Does she care?

Does the artist have a strong, stable work ethic? Does she overwork as a means of turning something she enjoys into something self-destructive? Does she transform her creative act into painful experience to avoid having to invest herself in it emotionally?

Is the artist open to working with other people? Is the artist open to criticism and critique, or is she oversensitive, defensive, and closed off? If she is defensive, is there a way to discuss and critique her work without straying into delicate territory and engaging her emotions and sensitivity?

Does the artist generally deflect any comments, kind words, or criticisms she receives?

Does the artist feel that her vision of her work is its absolute and only interpretation, or is she open to other people's interpretations of it? Is she confused about what that vision is? Can she be objective about the work, or it impossible for her to separate her ego from it?

When you speak to the artist, does she pay attention to what you are saying, or does she focus on specific points? Does she appear to "blank out" at certain points in a discussion as if she has shut down and is unable to process what you are saying? Does she only hear specific comments—positive or negative—that she wants to hear? Does she reconfigure the information and commentary you are directing toward her so it all fits into her worldview and perception of herself—is she a "selective listener"?

And there may be even more questions as the process develops.

DOES THE ARTIST RESPOND POSITIVELY OR NEGATIVELY TO THE FOLLOWING?

- Brutal criticism
- Honest, fair criticism
- Gentle criticism
- Suggestion
- Manipulation
- Encouragement
- Kindness
- Coddling
- Courtesy
- Attention
- Being ignored
- Fabrication
- Respect
- Empathy
- Sympathy
- Relaxation
- Love
- Some combination of all the above

ARTISTS ARE PEOPLE, TOO

Here are some general guidelines regarding how to coach, produce, and work with artists. Remember, always keep a clear head and be ready to take either a step backward or a step forward.

Make a point of *not* dictating to the artist. It's important to let him know that you look at the work you are doing together as a collaboration, not a manipulation or an effort to dominate or control him. Emphasize creative collaboration and avoid creating hierarchy between yourself and the artist. Maintain a relaxed creative relationship and avoid establishing yourself as a dictator.

You're attempting to earn the artist's trust in order to get the best results, not to turn the artist into an extension of yourself. Be careful of being overly negative around the artist or using negatively charged words, as they often sound like orders and may cause the artist to feel limited instead of free. With this in mind, it's helpful to avoid words such as "shouldn't," "don't," or "can't" when offering critiques or making suggestions to an artist. Words like these are very powerful and can establish a negative feeling in the creative space you both share.

When a creative choice must be made (such as altering one of the songs you will be recording), it is generally beneficial for you to appear impartial while still being supportive of the artist and taking an interest in him. Try sharing your objective perspective with the artist, present him with all the variables and options available, and then permit him to choose for himself. In most cases, he may ask which option you feel is most appropriate, and request that you make the choice based on your own experience or come up with a solution that is ideal for him.

Although this doesn't require open discussion, you're attempting to help the artist achieve breakthroughs so he can develop creatively. One way of encouraging this is by helping the artist become open and vulnerable with you. You can make him feel at ease by being relaxed, casual, and appropriately vulnerable—simply being yourself. Being relaxed around others often causes them to reciprocate in kind, and as the artist begins to open up, he will also be able to go deeper inside himself. He will become better able to access and utilize his deepest personal expression.

When an artist becomes vulnerable, there is a good chance he'll also be more emotionally delicate than normal and require being treated with extra consideration. You can perhaps empathize with how this vulnerable state feels by imagining such diverse sensory experiences as having a heightened sense of overall sensitivity, a feeling of euphoria, or an occasional burning sensation as if someone is vigorously rubbing sandpaper over your soul. Responding appropriately to this vulnerable state will sometimes require patience and delicacy from you; at other times, it will call for force and vigor.

By opening himself up, the artist is trusting you with his work, his feelings, and to an extent, his emotional well-being. (In a way, this process reminds me a bit of how an animal rolls onto his back and exposes his belly to you to demonstrate that he trusts you.) Because of this surrender, it helps to try empathizing with the artist and to imagine yourself in his shoes.

Consider the artist's feelings when you present him with ideas and commentary. By being sensitive to this (and perhaps imagining how you would feel if the roles were reversed and you were being critiqued), you will be better able to make your ideas more comprehensible, palatable, and acceptable to the artist. However, this doesn't mean that you should reserve your comments because you are afraid of hurting the artist's feelings. If you must say something that could possibly be perceived as inflammatory, it's usually best to select an opportune moment to have the conversation or take extra time to choose the right words.

By trusting your instincts and empathizing with the artist, you'll know what to say and how to say it. Empathy pertains to skill in both listening to someone else and "reading" or sensing his feelings. This can help your words make the greatest impact in the most productive manner and generate the most positive response.

Consistent reinforcement of ideas and information in a creative environment is also very important. Once a specific point is addressed to the artist (such as generalities in song writing, structure, personal health, or behavior), it is helpful to reaffirm it over time without making it tiresome.

Through your own consistent behavior, you can also encourage the artist to develop patience. Give him enough space to feel his own power, then take a step back and objectively observe his behavior, his humanity, and his flaws. You can do this by simply finding the neutral, calm space in yourself when the artist becomes reactive in a stressful situation, and by not reacting to or participating in his behavior. Offer him insight through your consistent example; in this way, he can experience how patience looks in action and gradually generate it on his own. The virtues of patience can also be discussed openly with the artist and reinforced through such disciplines as meditation.

In creative work, it is vitally important for the artist to learn to pace himself. Pacing is specific to each person, it can offer the artist unique insight into his own process and help him observe it more objectively.

Often, artists will casually knock their own work without considering the ramifications. You may need to explain to the artist how and when he cuts himself down, or uses derogatory or negative language to describe himself or his work. If you react consistently each time the artist displays this behavior, he will begin to notice when he is doing it. As the artist becomes aware of this behavior pattern, he will (with consistent positive reinforcement) gradually develop an aversion to it. He will also become more aware of his own subconscious actions and compulsions that stimulate this behavior.

As an example, I have noticed that artists with low self-esteem can be more self-deprecating, needy, and childlike and often seek more approval and affirmation when they feel sick or tired. I find that if this is pointed out (in a sensitive, nonjudgmental way) to an artist every time he feels ill and starts behaving this way, he will usually begin to notice it on his own.

As the artist becomes aware of his behavior patterns, he develops an understanding of how they affect him and he can make the choice to continue them or let them go. This awareness can also empower the artist and enhance his own sense of feeling in control of his process.

Teach through direction as well as by example; sometimes, you must be a leader. In all situations, it's important to follow the golden rule: do to others as you would have them do to you. This further reinforces a framework of consistency and provides a positive example for the artist.

A creative idea that you feel will benefit the artist can be made more compelling for him if you explain how it's also relevant to your own ethical code, beliefs, and feelings. It's easier to convince others that an idea is worth trying if you not only believe what you are preaching, but you also practice it.

Just as the artist must demonstrate to you that he is deserving of your attention, it is also reasonable that you do likewise for the artist. In order to prove to the artist that you deserve his trust and confidence, you must show him results. In my experience, it often takes three demonstrations of your ability as a producer to do this.

These demonstrations can be in the form of a musical or arrangement solution you provide for the artist's music; a behavioral aspect of the artist that you address (that is, properly identified and soothed or eased); or a solution you provide to a physical problem that is affecting the artist's performance. This shows the artist that you are able to contribute creatively and actively in the process.

The ability to pick up on physical and emotional "tells" is a valuable tool for the producer and is often cultivated by just being present and paying attention to what is happening in the immediate environment.

Often, when an artist presents his music for scrutiny, he either believes it is in the best shape possible or he can't imagine how it can possibly be improved. In spite of this, there are almost always structural or arrangement issues that need to be addressed.

By the very nature of his role in the creative process, the artist often can't be objective regarding his own work—nor should he be expected to. Because he has a more personal relationship to his work and requires assistance with it, he may get upset when critique comes from an outside source. This, in itself, may cause the artist to feel inadequate and perhaps to use this situation as a means to beat himself up emotionally (especially if he is naturally so inclined). He may feel bad because he didn't initially see the problem, which has been identified. This feeling may become further intensified because in his mind, he created something imperfect that must now be fixed. He may additionally feel inadequate because not only does he feel he created the problem but he was also unable to see the solution. In any case, he may feel hurt or behave in a defensive manner, even if a positive solution has been presented to him with no offense intended.

Pay close attention to what you say to the artist and how you say it. Pay close attention to the responses you receive from him.

In showing an artist how to experience his own work objectively (or to make it easier for him in permitting you to critique his work), approach making suggestions in a positive, calm, constructive manner so that they are easier for him to digest and can take root. Approaching an artist (or any creative work) in a demanding, insistent manner (or by employing persuasion or manipulation to force the artist's hand) can establish an unpleasant precedent in the creative process and potentially affect his openness to new ideas or critique in the future. He may retreat inward and shut down any progress you have made in drawing him out.

When working to reinforce an artist's objectivity, editing their work, applying constructive criticism, or encouraging them to accept new ideas, I often use William Faulkner's quote, "In writing, you must kill all your darlings." This statement adds a philosophical perspective to what can potentially be a very unpleasant process for the artist, and helps to objectify it for him. It also makes it easier for him to accept that careful examination and modification of his work can be both beneficial and necessary in the creative process, instead of being an underhanded insult to his ability.

You're not merely working with the artist—you're also establishing an unspoken contract with him. You're acknowledging that you appreciate the artist's talent, and this allows you to offer something beneficial to augment his work and take responsibility for your contribution to it. Sincerity and genuine enthusiasm are true gifts that, when shared with other people, are very powerful, contagious, and motivational.

Similarly, by choosing to work with you, the artist is accepting another unspoken agreement. Without being consciously aware, he is preparing to open himself up and go as far as he needs to in order to achieve what he needs to. Your responsibility is to provide the motivation, inspiration, and direction.

Generally, about 50 percent of your job is done the moment the artist chooses to work with you. After this, it is up to you to demonstrate through the application of your skills that you are worthy of the artist's trust and respect.

Each project and artist has different needs. Some require tight structure and organization in order to generate maximum productivity; others function best with virtually no structure. You must decide which approach is best, based on what you observe and how the artist cues you.

Once a project gets rolling, creative situations often take on a life of their own. The creative process is an organic and living entity that functions on its own energy and controls the players, instead of the other way around. The creative process defies and deftly defeats the egotistical goals of those who desperately need to control every situation.

If you try to control or dominate a creative process once it has begun to unfold, you'll be defeated. If you trust and let go, the process itself will know what to do. It always does.

Although production consists of multiple techniques, it works better when those techniques are not applied rigidly or systematically. No two creative situations are, or should be, treated the same. Because production is intended to address the unique needs of each artist, it is best not to follow a strict template. It is more important to be aware of what you experience when you are in a room working with an artist or listening to his music. Approaching your role in this way makes you more flexible and creative.

Find a general guideline, specific to the artist, and keep the process between you engaging, fresh, and in some ways, consistent—yet occasionally unpredictable. It's important to keep the creative process from getting stale, because artists are highly sensitive, intelligent, and often extremely analytical. Being so analytical, they are constantly and subconsciously seeking familiar patterns—in work, behavior, people, and other areas. If the artist feels he understands or has analyzed your process, he can become distracted and bored (instead of remaining open) and you might lose him.

It is important to pace the process while also relying upon spontaneity. Work with the unknown and the unexpected, allowing them to become teaching tools.

As the process unfolds, you may experience in yourself a diminished access to certain teaching or training skills that you often find useful, and a heightened access to others. This is nothing more than a means of guiding you to the skills you will need for each unique creative situation.

The importance of originality in one's personal expression can't be understated. Discussing this is valuable; however, it is easy to fall into a rut by only addressing it verbally. The creative space can become too cerebral, and the visceral nature of creativity is gradually forgotten if there is too much talking and not enough doing.

Demonstrating ideas (or sensory examples combined with verbal communication) can sometimes get them across with more impact. For example, you can use examples of what you are talking about to demonstrate how an abstract concept (personal expression, originality, and the quest to find one's true voice) actually manifests in concrete terms.

One way to do this might be establishing a relative context between the artist you're working with and another, perhaps better-known artist. For instance, the artist you're working with might not make music like Frank Sinatra's; however, he can listen to Sinatra's work as a general point of reference for such things as vocal phrasing, expression, and tone. As another example, the artist's music might not sound like Led Zeppelin; however, he can listen to Led Zeppelin's music as a point of reference for instrument relationships, interdependent playing, and "feel." Cross-referencing the artist's music with other musical references that the artist identifies with, feels a relationship to, or admires is one way to help him be more flexible and open to change. Another way is to cross-reference the artist's original demo recordings with newer versions of his songs as they are being modified. This can also help to expand his perspective regarding his work.

Context, points of reference, and comparison are useful tools for analyzing an artist's work. Discussing the lives and work of great artists sets a standard and creates a unique context for the artist to view his own work. By recontextualizing and altering the artist's creative landscape, you are helping the artist to grow creatively. You are essentially creating a kind of "cognitive dissonance" for the artist.

I love the concept of cognitive dissonance. In the case of working with an artist, cognitive dissonance can be the result of anything that forces the artist outside of his comfort zone into unknown and potentially threatening territory. With no map, compass, or sense of direction, he must operate without the intellectual process he has come to rely upon—by instinct alone. This winds up being potentially terrifying, but ultimately, it may be the most liberating thing that can happen to him.

There are many ways to draw the artist out of his comfort zone. Because the mind depends on familiarity as a means of survival and to keep from feeling insane, it can be helpful to find ways to destabilize the artist's sense of order. If an artist has gotten comfortable with how you and he interact, try changing this, just to see the effect it has on his creativity.

One idea is playing recordings for the artist of music forms that are completely alien to him. Listening to ethnic and folk music from other cultures, religious music, ritual music, and music that accompanies social activities in indigenous societies is fascinating and can create a sensation of cognitive dissonance so powerful that it resembles taking a consciousness-altering drug. Encountering music that was created and performed by people who possess no other agenda than the need to express themselves (by way of something specific to their culture and incredibly foreign to ours) can be a life-changing experience for someone who has been led to believe he must make music in order to have a hit record.

There are sensory experiences that can put an artist into direct contact with his own body as a kind of somatic tool. The use of Tibetan singing bowls and tuning forks, for example, applied directly to the body can help shut down the cerebral part of the creative process, leaving only the sensory, nonrational part.

Other ways of altering the artist's sense of reality and perspective are to expose him to unusual modes of expression and modes of visual, such as performance art, installation pieces, and so on. Altering his sense of reality can help demonstrate to the artist that perception is subjective, and that to grow creatively, it can be beneficial for him to reconsider his own perception of what he does. This can have far-reaching effects and may go straight to the core of his fundamental belief system.

The ability to view his work in new contexts and from new perspectives can help the artist assess his own work objectively.

Change is often scary, but always necessary.

Changing the working environment is another means to alter perception. Doing creative work in unorthodox locales such as beaches, public areas, train stations, apartments, and vacant buildings is one way to keep the creative experience fresh and constantly stimulating. Simply being present right where one is at any given moment is another. Moving objects around in a familiar place, engaging in another completely different activity (which is stimulating in some way) prior to working, and doing role-play exercises are also helpful.

You can also act as a mirror for the artist. By describing, exemplifying, and identifying to him what is so unique about what he does, you can help the artist understand more about his own abilities from a completely objective, yet positive and supportive perspective. His self-perception may be distorted, but because he has chosen to work with you (and is gradually learning to trust you), he looks to you for honesty. When you offer him your observations about him that are out of sync with his self-perception, this creates a powerful experience of cognitive dissonance. Offering him your perspective can help dissipate negative associations the artist might have experienced previously.

Depending on how receptive he is you can introduce the artist to various forms of bodywork, such as exercise, yoga, breathing, meditation, and healing. This will help him develop a deeper relationship with his body as a device in his creative toolkit, as well as connecting him to the physical sensations that he relates to the process of creativity, itself.

Discipline can be very helpful for an artist and often manifests through physical activity and bodywork. Artists with a prior background in athletics have a tremendous advantage here, as they are often well disciplined and good at working under pressure and meeting deadlines.

Hard work always pays off, but everyone needs breaks and some artists need more breaks than others. This could be for a variety of reasons: perhaps their attention begins to wander over time, or they may have a physical issue that causes them discomfort. Depending on the artist, it is helpful to either schedule breaks or simply call them when the time feels right. Scheduled breaks are helpful for those artists who require structure. Unscheduled breaks are perfect for artists who prefer a looser working environment.

For individuals with back problems, it is ideal to stand up every forty-five minutes to an hour in order to straighten out and loosen up. Light stretching and exercise is also helpful.

Analyzing and rebuilding the artist's music can be drudgery, or it can be a stimulating and fun experience. The process of revisiting and reworking a piece of music sometimes causes an artist to be uncomfortable. This may be because the artist sees this process as potentially being insurmountably hard work (and again, the act of revising their work may somehow suggest to them that they have created something that isn't perfect).

As the process unfolds and the artist gradually understands that revising his music is necessary and normal and that his input is essential to this process, he will choose to be more involved. Until that point is reached, you—as producer—are the individual in this process with the most experience. Therefore, it is up to you to make the process stimulating (and enjoyable) for the artist and yourself.

DISTRACTIONS ARE DETRIMENTAL TO GOOD WORK. WITH THIS IN MIND . . .

- Avoid discussing other projects or artists you are working with. If you are asked, be brief and as general as possible. Everyone has their own insecurities and generally wants to feel that they are the sole recipients of your attention.

- Punctuality is very important. Being on time demonstrates professional courtesy, self-respect, and respect for others. Lateness doesn't look or feel good to people you're working with.

- An artist doesn't care if you are feeling sick, dealing with personal issues, or tired. Unless you are too debilitated to work (in which case, it is best to cancel until you feel well), even if he likes some drama in his own life, he doesn't really want to hear about your problems. By complaining, you are injecting your own ego into the creative space and adversely affecting everyone around you.

- Avoid making inquiries into (or getting involved in) the artist's personal life unless it's absolutely relevant to your work or can provide a deeper understanding into his creative process. Anything else is unnecessary and intrusive. By focusing on personal details, you are inviting the artist to derail his own creative process by adding or amplifying drama in his life and adversely affecting his attention span.

- In the interest of maintaining consistency and avoiding distractions, it is always best to keep your personal life out of the creative space you share with the artist unless it is somehow relevant or beneficial to the work being done.

No matter what the artist's expectations are of you, it is important to remain consistent regarding how you view your function in the creative process. Whether the artist wants you to be domineering or submissive in relation to him, you're always better off being neutral and not accommodating any other expectations.

This is another reason it benefits you to assess and be aware of your immediate environment on a regular basis. It is also important to be aware of your own feelings, neuroses, urges, and impulses in order to properly engage with an artist when you feel any disconnect in communication between you.

When too much of your own ego starts to infiltrate a creative work environment, you inadvertently begin to dominate it, and both the artist and you lose out. Instead, by keeping your ego in check and maintaining a neutral demeanor, you can affect the process in a more productive manner and simultaneously expand the space the artist needs to do his work optimally. For example, if you are having a conversation, this can often be achieved by letting the artist do most of the talking while you do the listening.

While it's possible to improve something you don't like or that isn't very good, you can only make something truly great if you feel connected to it and love it passionately. For this reason, it is best to work with artists who have obvious and recognizable creative ability, are expressive and open to expanding their range and capabilities to the fullest (and have the drive to make this a reality), and with whom you feel a strong personal connection or whose work you truly love. If you feel this intrinsic connection at any level, this is a strong indicator that you are going in the right direction.

Be ready and willing to work for the benefit of the creative process itself without letting your ego or a personal agenda interfere with the process. If you are open to this as one of your prime directives, it is important that you check yourself regularly and examine your own motives in the creative process. Self-assessment also helps maintain your sensitivity to intuit or "feel" the artist's work and state of mind. Are you able to put your own petty interests aside for an ethical position, an ideal, or someone else's needs, and listen to what your body tells you, instead of serving a personal agenda?

Eliminating your need for control can help you maintain your objectivity when you work creatively with others.

By accepting the role of producer, you will probably assume a proprietary attitude toward an artist's work at some point in the creative process. Conversely, by selecting you to produce his work, the artist is acknowledging this and offering you a degree of propriety, at least while the project is ongoing.

With this propriety comes power, and with power must also come objectivity, accountability, and responsibility. Keeping this in mind, you can consider yourself the artist's conscience. In assuming this role, you must sometimes anticipate what will be best for him—even if it may seem unpleasant. Sometimes kindness is the best way to encourage greatness in the artist, and sometimes toughness is the best road to take.

Consider what the terms *good* and *bad* mean to you. Although they are subjective in nature, they can be applicable when you are working to improve a piece of music. The concepts of good and bad can be anchored to sensory experiences in order to use them referentially when listening to music. Try and use your body as a sensory device in order to judge what feels good or bad to you with greater acuity.

As previously stated, ideas occasionally require revising or reworking. This is usually determined by hearing a piece of music and noticing where the music feels "bad" to you, or where you are having trouble paying attention to it.

Sometimes, the original placement of an idea in a piece of music is ideal and requires no repair. This is generally the case when something that occurred spontaneously can't be improved upon and, on further consideration, is already perfect.

Of course, this should not be used as an excuse to avoid restructuring or rearranging a piece of work that may need help.

Encourage the artist to take risks, and applaud him for his effort, even if he fails. Success is a wonderful reward, but failure is a great teacher. If an artist doesn't feel safe while aspiring to greatness, working hard, and taking great risks, he will be unable to experience his full creative range. Absent this, he will never live up to his full potential and, consequently, will miss his opportunity to be a truly great artist. In order to experience his full range, he must also experience failure because, without it, he will never fully comprehend success.

Encourage the artist to explore every aspect of his psyche— unpleasant and pleasant. This is one of the best ways he can expand his creative range. And it will be a constant source of fresh inspiration.

Invite the artist to learn the rules and technique of his chosen discipline in order to bend the rules, violate technique, and shred the playbook. This is where the artist can find his own power and individuality.

Be attentive to interpersonal dynamics between the musicians. Be conscious of not becoming engaged in any preexisting issues between them—always remain on the outside. By not engaging in these relationships, you will be able to bring stability and functionality to the proceedings. The other participants will observe your behavior and learn from the example it sets.

In a collaborative environment, it is important for you to accept compliments from others. It is also important to compliment others for their efforts. When an artist has made a particularly strong effort or done good work, it helps to recognize this and openly acknowledge it to him without being patronizing or fake.

In everything you do, find the ease. Just remember, ease is not always easy. Getting things to flow is often the result of consciously investing yourself in a process and then allowing that process to operate on its own. Once things begin to flow, they work on their own.

The creative process always begins by your invoking it; then you step back and allow it to take over. In a sense it's a lot like casting a magical spell and letting powers beyond your understanding run rampant while transforming everything and everyone in the vicinity. How could anything be better than that?

BEHAVIORAL ISSUES—WATCH OUT!

Here are some warning signs I've encountered that indicate an artist has difficulty moving past her own issues. I've seen these indicators in both individuals and in groups.

- The artist is very insecure about her own creative work and her decisions. She constantly second-guesses her choices and is unwilling (or unable) to rely on her own judgment.
- The artist is constantly in a state of agitation and nervous energy.
- The artist is afraid of success.
- The artist is afraid of failure.
- The artist is afraid of her immediate environment.
- The artist is afraid of disappointing others.
- The artist is afraid of the art form she works in.
- The artist is afraid of committing to something and often seems too paralyzed to act.
- The artist has poor time-management skills—personally and creatively.
- The artist overthinks everything, especially small details, such as meal choices.
- The artist has a constant and obsessive need to figure things out, or to understand them intellectually. It may be easier for her to accept what she's doing if she can understand it as a mental construct or a mechanical function, instead of something innate and mysterious that can't be controlled.
- The artist feels the need to push or muscle through every situation, often without being aware of what she is doing, considering why she is doing it, or what the potential consequences of her actions might be.
- The artist has an obsessive need to be accepted and liked. She looks for acceptance mainly from authority figures and transposed parental figures. She may often try to change who she is and what she does to gain acceptance.

- The artist may push people away who offer to help her because she is suspicious of them for liking her. She may also push people away because she feels they will inevitably reject her and she would rather reject them first.
- The artist has unresolved issues regarding disapproval she received from her parents. This can often manifest in a dislike or disdain for authority figures (in this case, represented by the producer).
- The artist is unfamiliar with feeling comfortable in her own skin. She often avoids comfort or anything that might be soothing.
- The artist avoids anything that could make her creative process easier. She can't conceive of ease or of anything being easy for her and, therefore, doesn't trust that anything is.
- The artist feels as though she doesn't deserve attention. She is terrified of being seen by others and is afraid that she may be revealed as a fake or untalented.
- The artist needs authority figures to enable her or make her feel whole. She acts helpless and establishes a passive-aggressive dynamic with authority figures.
- The artist has accumulated a large amount of unfinished work that consistently grows larger, because finishing something would mean she'd have to commit to it. She feels safer in a state of paralysis.

These Behaviors Can Be Triggered When...

- The artist has long periods of no work, respite, or inactivity during a project.
- The artist encounters critique or criticism of any kind.

- The artist imagines criticism or critique even when none has been given.
- The artist experiences self-doubt or other random stimuli that induce self-doubt.
- The artist becomes panicked that she has missed a vital piece of information or instruction, or misunderstood something without which she will be completely lost.
- The artist takes undue responsibility for random technical issues that normally occur over the course of a recording, even though she did not cause them. When something completely out of her control goes wrong, she reacts as if she is somehow at fault.
- The artist begins to self-assess and self-criticize her work and performance as a means she has used in the past to belittle herself.
- Without being provoked, the artist compares herself disparagingly to other similar artists. I think of this as a creativity dysmorphism because of the destructive nature of comparing one's self to someone else through a distorted lens.
- The artist feels like a victim and expresses incredulity that she hasn't acquired management or been signed by a record company (although there are often good reasons for this).

SIGNS THAT AN ARTIST IS POTENTIALLY SELF-DESTRUCTIVE

These are some indicators I've encountered in artists that either led to problems in a creative environment or, in the worst-case scenario, to a finished recording that was far less than it could have been.

- From 50 to 100 percent of the artist's songs are unfinished when they are initially presented to be produced.
- The artist shows signs or has a history of drug or alcohol abuse.
- The artist has poor or no impulse control.
- The artist is unable to keep his promises, work to deadlines, or finish anything he starts.
- The artist obsessively prioritizes other things (such as drug usage, extracurricular work, other interests, or other people) before creative work.
- The artist consistently and obsessively diverts attention in the creative space away from work and toward himself and things that have nothing to do with creative work. He displays unpredictable, disruptive behavior that interferes with everyone else's workflow.
- The artist obsessively diverts attention to superficial aspects of himself (such as his appearance or other business interests) and away from meaningful aspects or deep personal feelings. He fixates on things (often illusory or imaginary) and prioritizes them over his talent and everything he excels at.
- The artist is open to addressing a specific problem he has but treats it lightly or laughs it off as if the problem is trivial and will go away if he ignores or avoids it.
- The artist talks about his problems as if they belong to someone else.
- The artist has an apparent lack of interest in his creative work and commits a minimal investment of time and effort to it.

It suddenly becomes difficult for anyone else to concentrate or focus on creative work when the artist enters the creative space. This is because certain artists have what I call "the power to cloud men's minds." In extreme cases, people with this ability can even cause equipment to malfunction by simply being around it. And, although it sounds like an episode of "Paranormal Record Production," I have actually seen this happen.

HOW TO DEAL WITH ARTISTS WHO ARE "UNHINGED"

Over the years, I have encountered a wide variety of unusual and "colorful" artists. Some are utterly driven and will let absolutely nothing stand between them and their vision. Others also have a powerful creative vision but frequently allow their mental process and/or erratic behavior to interfere with its expression.

And then there are those artists who, for whatever reason, are generally considered absolutely impossible to work with. These are the artists with reputations for such things as substance abuse, throwing tantrums, and being extremely abusive and even violent to coworkers, employees, and random bystanders.

In the course of any creative endeavor, you will probably come across an individual like this. You'll know in advance what to expect from him, because he is preceded by his history of erratic behavior. Unfortunately, other people may see this behavior as his primary distinguishing characteristic—part of his charisma, above and beyond whatever talent he possesses.

In many cases, people who possess a hair-trigger temper or who flip out with little or no provocation have a low tolerance to stress. Their behavior may also be triggered by low blood sugar, overwork, or lack of sleep. They are often used to living with these conditions (albeit erratically) and have found no need to mitigate them.

Some individuals like this are aware of their own temperament but feel that is simply how they express themselves. Others behave this way because they enjoy throwing their weight around and bullying others. These individuals will often put themselves in a position of power by making themselves indispensible in some way and then acting out to prove that they can dominate the situation as they wish.

People who throw fits are used to others responding to their outbursts in one of three general ways: backing down entirely from the confrontation, attempting to coddle the individual having the meltdown, or meeting him or her with aggression. Needless to say, reacting to this behavior in any way never works.

I have found that when anyone on a recording project throws a temper tantrum, it is best to adopt a zero-tolerance policy. For me, "zero-tolerance" means either letting the individual who is throwing the tantrum know that they're permitted only one opportunity to behave in this fashion around me (and they have just used that opportunity up), disengaging entirely from the creative process until the incident has been dealt with conclusively, or dismissing the individual in question on the spot.

However, it is only useful to practice the zero-tolerance approach if you are comfortable with potentially ending your working relationship with the individual throwing the tantrum (since people who throw tantrums generally don't like being told that they're behaving in an unacceptable manner). They also don't like being told what to do, and they don't like it when they've lost control of a situation (which, in this case, is manifested by someone telling them, in no uncertain terms, that their behavior is unacceptable). Dealing directly with a person in this condition can potentially bring your involvement with her to a screeching halt.

Now, what happens if the person throwing a tantrum is someone who is indispensible to the project you're working on—or is even the principal artist? In this case, you may probably have put a great deal of effort into the project and you don't want to see it all evaporate in one poorly thought-out move. In this instance, you may find yourself in a dilemma.

Even though the artist's behavior is completely unacceptable and makes you feel as though you're being physically assaulted, you don't want to abandon your commitment to your project or the time you've already invested. You want to regain some balance so that things can settle back to normal and the work can continue. Additionally, you don't want the tension to escalate beyond where it already is. Your mind may be racing, because confrontation often causes adrenaline to flow into the body and induces a fight-or-flight state.

Instead of reacting—submissively or aggressively—the best thing to do is to find neutrality. Maintain your composure and use your intuition to get a read of the situation. Sometimes high-strung individuals and those with no ability to handle stress may actually be seeking approval but do this in a very unorthodox and off-putting way when they are stressed. Others behave in an infantile or belligerent manner to determine who in the creative space is the alpha dog. They are testing the waters to see if you can lead them, or if they can lead you.

Whatever kind of person you are dealing with, slow down, take some deep breaths, and mentally distance yourself from what is taking place. This requires shutting your own emotions down and watching any unfolding drama from a purely analytical and objective viewpoint. When you breathe out, imagine that you're releasing all of the tension and anger that may be building up inside of you. As you do this, the fight-or-flight response and any impulse to respond in anger will gradually fade away.

When someone you are doing intense creative work with has a fit and directs it your way, the first impulse is usually to react to them in direct proportion. Because a tantrum is expressed aggressively, you may initially experience an impulse to defend yourself and respond aggressively in return.

Reacting aggressively to aggression often escalates a situation like this into a full confrontation. To avoid this, when the impulse to react arises in you, it helps to first objectify the feeling and observe it as something separate from you, instead of as a very powerful emotion that you could potentially let control you. From there, the impulse becomes easier to suppress as it gradually abates.

Assuming that the individual in question has a low tolerance to stress, try letting the situation dissipate on its own. People who blow up in this fashion often just need to vent and only have very primitive means to do so. It's generally not meant as a personal attack, even if it's directed at you specifically.

By reacting to a tantrum, you are not only providing traction to the person who is having it, but you are also diverting him from being able to vent (which itself may be the underlying cause of the histrionics and will undoubtedly exacerbate him). In a sense, being reactive to the tantrum is somewhat akin to waking a sleepwalker from sleep: the sleepwalker's response can be violent.

It may be helpful to see this person as someone who is momentarily lost, perhaps even completely panicked for any number of reasons. For that matter, she may be completely over-stimulated, and losing control is her way to reestablish normalcy.

Let her get everything out that she needs to—let the situation be a monologue without turning it into a dialogue. Remember, this explosion is not about you; it is exclusively about the person throwing the tantrum.

Be aware of your intent, keep breathing slowly with ease, stay calm and still your mind. Relax all the muscles in your body, let your arms hang by your sides, be loose and comfortable—move as little as possible without being rigid. Look directly at her while she speaks, but not in her eyes as this can be perceived as a provocation or challenge. Maintain your physical proximity to her without moving around, and give her all the space you feel she needs. By offering space but not moving, you are establishing that you are respectful but unafraid.

Let her finish venting—you will know when she is done because she will either wind down or leave the immediate vicinity. It takes a lot of effort to vent, and once that has subsided, it often requires more energy than she's capable of exerting to continue. If she leaves, it is probably best to let her be alone until she is ready to interact again. If she stays in the room, she may be looking for a resolution or some affirmation that although she behaved inappropriately, things are okay.

If she addresses you or asks you a question while she's still venting, it's best to respond slowly and gently using a few mono-syllabic words. Be thoughtful in your delivery and choose your words with intent. This will make it easier for her to process what you are saying and will anchor her, acting as a contrast to her own behavior. As you are speaking, you can sense whether it is helpful to move closer to her in order to help her feel more comfortable, or to maintain distance. If she moves toward you as she is winding down, this may be a way of gaining approval, a positive affirmation or conciliation. If your goal is to keep the peace, let her have it. Your intuition will tell you what you need to do.

Once the episode has ended, it's generally best to let it go and not discuss it. If you have any residual feelings of anger, or leftover adrenaline, you might want to take a stroll someplace private and breathe it all out. Ideally, you will remain placid and pleasant, in direct contrast to what has happened. The contrast of calm versus hysteria is uncomfortable and by creating it, you are helping this person learn for herself that her behavior is unacceptable and doesn't benefit her.

Being in the presence of someone throwing a tantrum can become an endurance test, especially if she is excessively abusive, menacing, and/or violent. As important as it is to be mindful, patient, and maintain order through example, it is also important to establish and maintain boundaries with others. Exuding confidence and compassion in a creative space is a positive way to express that you have boundaries and they may not be crossed. If the artist behaves unacceptably on multiple occasions or breeches a boundary that you consider sacred, you will know that it's time to deal with the situation more stringently.

Generally, if an individual throws a tantrum once, chances are it will happen again. A recurrence may be a further reaction to stress, chemical, or environmental issues, or it may simply be a situation where the artist has already done this once and wants to see if she can get away with it again.

Knowing that the potential for another blowup is always on the table, it helps to maintain calm while being patient and keeping an eye out at all times. Being consistently respectful and thoughtful to one's coworkers gives them less traction and makes it harder for them to behave aggressively unless they are really looking to start a fight.

In addition, it is important to recognize when one person's narcissism is holding everyone else in the creative space hostage. This is absolutely unacceptable and must be addressed immediately.

On a rare occasion, someone will throw a tantrum in order to escalate into a physical altercation. This kind of behavior is a deal breaker under any circumstances and should bring the creative process to a grinding halt.

WHEN IT'S TIME TO STOP RESCUING AN ARTIST

Once upon a time, I produced a record that began coming apart at the seams. I will leave out the gory details, names, and specifics, but suffice it to say that drama infused this project on an epic scale, from drugs to mental illness to misappropriated funds to occasional appearances by law enforcement, etcetera, etcetera, ad infinitum. At the epicenter of all this mayhem (and, not surprisingly, its very source) was the artist I was producing. This project had started out reasonably well, plateaued for a short time, and suddenly, went straight into a nosedive when the artist's varied predilections for self-destruction quickly began to infiltrate every nook and cranny of the project. I found myself hanging on by a thread while trying to rescue the artist. The artist, meanwhile, had spiraled out of control on a crazy train and was taking everyone else in the immediate vicinity along for the ride. As one of those unfortunates, I tried to hang on for as long as I could. I felt responsible for the project and the artist, but it gradually became apparent that the cost of that feeling was becoming too high.

The work stopped; there was nothing to produce. The artist was completely absorbed in all manner of unpleasant diversions, had disengaged completely from recording, and as the project lost its direction, so did I. After the stress of it all started getting to me, I finally realized that things on this project would never improve. This artist was lost in the ether and I couldn't be the white knight anymore.

I saw my choice: either stay and continue to watch things fall apart, or leave and feel better. The choice was simple—I left.

Prior to that, I had worked on a different project—one in which the artist was also self-destructing—his love of heroin was sucking the life out of him and everything in his immediate vicinity. Drastic steps were needed to salvage whatever remained before this guy flushed both his career and his life down the toilet.

The only reason the project was eventually finished and the artist became stratospherically successful was through the force of his own will. There were mighty demons playing havoc with his soul, but in the end he was strong enough to prioritize his work over the impulse to self-destruct. He pulled himself out of his free fall. His work was all he had, and he knew he needed it far more than he needed his drug addiction.

A true artist is able to dig deep into the wellspring of his own experience so he can create something magical and powerful.

This source is the place inside himself where he goes so he can connect with other people on the deepest possible level.

The flip side is that the waters of this wellspring are often very bitter. It can be extraordinarily painful to go to this place, and an artist who is already incredibly sensitive will feel this pain far more intensely than most other people.

Of course, it is the artist's job to feel, to experience his emotions and report them with clarity so the rest of the world might share them or come into a deeper relationship with their own. An artist is the transcriber of his feelings, and the best artists do this with great accuracy, singularity, and intensity.

Because they are constantly engaged between emotional extremes, because they are acquainted so intimately with the outermost boundaries of existence, many artists develop an obsession with first finding the edge, and then pushing themselves well past it. This can manifest itself in poor impulse control, highly addictive behavior, and quite often, the urge to be self-destructive.

Many creative people I've worked with possessed some type of addiction or self-destructive tendency. The degree to which this was an issue was the degree to which each artist allowed it to enter the creative space and interfere with his (and everyone else's) work.

Many artists are able to keep their addictions and self-destructive issues in check, out of the spotlight, and away from their creative life. This is because they know that this sort of behavior will ultimately have a negative effect on their work. In many cases, they have already witnessed firsthand the havoc that their addictions (as well as many well-publicized addictions of other artists) can wreak and are cognizant enough to be able to prioritize their work over their personal issues. Sadly, not all are as perceptive or strong willed. Working with talented people can occasionally be as heartbreaking as it can be uplifting.

Being in the presence of a great artist who is digging deep into the recesses of his soul and expressing himself with total abandon is as near to a religious experience as one will likely get in this existence. On the other hand, there are few things more agonizing than witnessing the wasted ability of artists who are almost unfairly, disproportionately gifted, and yet allow themselves to be consumed by their addictions and choose the path of self-destruction over channeling themselves into their pure, natural talent.

It's kind of shocking and gives you pause. Wow, you think, this person has been given so much and he's taking every last drop of it for granted, just throwing it all away. How dare he spit in God's eye and disrespect that same inconceivable power that chose to bestow this great gift upon him?

Thinking this thought pisses you off at the artist. It also makes you want to save him.

Which also makes you want to control him.

But attempting to control someone else in this situation is an exercise in futility. The truth is, control can't be taken in a creative environment; it can only be surrendered. You can't help or save a person who doesn't want to be helped or saved. People will only listen to reason if they have convinced themselves beforehand that they need to hear it. Reasonable words, however well spoken, fall flawlessly on the deaf ears of fools.

It's often difficult to see the warning signs when an artist has a dangerous agenda that he prioritizes over his creative work. It's so much easier to perceive artists in the most flattering light, to see their talent and their limitless potential.

And for many of us, being around someone so talented and so damaged has its allure. You look upon the artist's beautiful brokenness and without even knowing it you get hooked instantly. You begin to crave this feeling like a drug and feed yourself the grand old lie that, with all the people the artist has had around him, he has never had anyone who could be as pragmatic, as truthful, or as compassionate as you. The yen gets worse and you tell yourself, this person needs me.

I can save him.

It's just too agonizingly sexy to let the mind run wild and imagine what greatness could be achieved by putting this broken person back together. Oh, the glory that could be yours and yours alone.

When that line gets crossed, seduction and ego triumph over pragmatism. And why not? One of the most important aspects of record production is maximizing the potential of incredibly talented individuals—no matter how savage and persistent their demons might be.

That's because a record producer is supposed to help take an artist higher, to his greatest glory. This is also because, as a record producer, it's a badge of merit to proclaim loud and clear to anyone within earshot that you're the one who turned loony into lucre. The room gets quiet, people look at you with big doe eyes, and in low, quavering, bucktoothed, cartoon character voices straight out of *Looney Tunes*, pose the question, "Uuhhhhh...gosh, how did yuh do it?"

When, of course, all you're really trying to tell them is that your balls are bigger than theirs.

Perhaps the safest way to envision working with an artist who may self-destruct at any moment is to pretend that you're riding a rocket. You prepare accordingly, strap yourself in, blast off, and pray to God that either you land someplace safe and sound—or that you manage to bail out right before the thing crashes.

But there finally comes a time when you must look at things through the cold, hard lens of reality and accept that there is nothing you or anyone else can do—or could have done—to save this person or their project. They must walk their own path, and somewhere down the line you have confused their path with your own. You realize that you seduced yourself into working with someone who is talented beyond anything reasonable or fair, but never had any intention of utilizing even a fraction of that mighty gift.

You can see now that you've been chasing a dragon—propping up the artist to fulfill your own unrealistic expectation of who he is or what he could be. You've been dealing with an adult child all this time—someone who has taken advantage of your best efforts so he could avoid being responsible for his life and his work. He read you like a book from the very first instant and used your ambition to hoist you on your own petard. It's that same old codependent song-and-dance routine, and you fell for it.

This is the moment when it's time to get real. This is the moment when it's time to let the artist go and to save yourself.

BODY/SENSORY AWARENESS AND HOW IT RELATES TO CREATIVE WORK

The mind is the realm of consciousness, but the body is the realm of sensation. The body has great value as a learning device and a creative tool because of its responsiveness to various stimuli.

However, it is difficult to consistently remain in *body awareness*, mainly because the mind is so powerful and we rely on it for so much.

As a producer, I feel that my role is also encouraging the artist to disengage from the cerebral approach she takes to her work and to help her embrace a deeper expressive, emotional, intuitive, physical sensory awareness. To do this, it is often necessary to move her out of the safety of her mind and into the uncharted wilderness of her body and her subconscious.

Meditation is a simple and easy way to relieve stress, relax, and develop body awareness. Exercise is also useful as a body awareness technique because, when exercising, you must often concentrate on the area of your body you are working. When you focus on your body to perform an exercise, since you can't focus on two things at once, this can stop the mind from working. People who are used to thinking obsessively often experience their brain quieting down as a loss of control or an extreme sense of discomfort (and that may explain why they may have difficulty remaining focused on exercising or meditating).

Bodywork and healing techniques include sound therapy (which involves playing tuned copper or crystal bowls), Reiki, acupuncture, tai chi, qi gong, and various forms of massage. As with meditation, these techniques can create a state of extreme relaxation and help achieve an enhanced experience of somatic awareness.

A healthy diet, adequate nourishment, and rest are essential to sustain a consistent workflow (and to enhance your body awareness). The human body is a powerful organism, but it has a limited amount of energy with which to do all the multitasking we demand of it. Often, you may be digesting a meal, resisting an infection, and doing something that demands a degree of physical exertion (such as walking someplace), in addition to the various autonomic functions in the body, as well as mental exertion and stress—and all this at the same time. Although this is commonplace and generally done unconsciously, such multitasking actually puts a tremendous drain on the body's energetic resources.

Where your body is concerned, it's important to apply these and other techniques moderately and not push too hard. Overdoing anything may cause discomfort, and discomfort often creates a negative association with whatever you're doing. If you repeat anything enough times in a way that feels unpleasant, you will create an aversion to doing it and, eventually, stop altogether.

When doing creative work, it's imperative that you're aware of your energy level. Without adequate energy, you will begin to function at a subpar level creatively, physically, mentally, and emotionally.

Diminished energy levels can generally be replenished by taking occasional short breaks from work, resting, napping briefly, and eating healthy meals. Although creative work is very inspiring, it can also be very tiring and tends to deplete creative individuals very quickly.

Adequate rest is another important part of maintaining balance in creative work. As with hunger, inadequate rest contributes to low energy, diminished expressive and technical capabilities, and diminished decision-making abilities. The only remedy for inadequate rest is getting enough sleep and rest until the artist is physically and mentally able to work again.

Proper rest and sustenance are crucial aspects of balance. They also influence physical resistance to illness and overall good health. Because creativity and musical performance are physical activities—inasmuch as both require optimal body function—they can become debilitating to an artist whose physical resistance and physical condition are poor.

It is ideal to take regular breaks every three hours (more or less) and cool down while doing creative work. Take a few minutes to get out of doors. If there is access to sunlight, this is very helpful, as it is an excellent source of vitamin D3.

While work is in progress, it is important to occasionally check in with the artist. When you sense she might need to idle for a little while, ask her how she's feeling, whether she's rested enough, when her last meal was, and if she's hungry. Making these inquiries gives the artist a sense of foundation, confidence in the process, and assuredness that you care about her physical well-being. It also gives you a deeper understanding of how the artist is feeling, how aware she is of her health, and how receptive she is to having other people take an interest in her. Eventually, as the artist sees that your concern for her physical needs has positive results, she may begin to take care of herself without any prompting.

As with most things, the body requires balance to be optimally functional, and balance is generally found in moderation. If the artist is open to learning about her body as a sensory receptor as well as a physical mechanism and the vessel she inhabits, she will learn how far it can be pushed and still function optimally, and it will serve her better as a creative mechanism.

6

MEDITATION
AND RELAXATION

The brain is an important component in the creative process, and it gets a lot of wear. While you're busy with your day, your brain is constantly in the background processing information, doing computations and probability gymnastics regarding everything from how you'll respond to a question about a song structure to what you want to eat for dinner.

It's a lot—after all these years working in recording studios, I still can never figure out what I want to eat for dinner.

The brain is also at the mercy of the many chemicals it regulates and secretes. Not only is it amazing that the brain distributes such a variety of potent hormonal cocktails, it's also amazing that with so many of these chemical concoctions the brain is relatively functional at all. With all the crazy things that people do, I often wonder if proper brain functionality is the exception and not the rule.

The brain is not infallible and requires maintenance like any other part of the body. It is easy to not be aware of this, precisely because the brain is the engine of awareness, and by its nature, it is more difficult to be objectively aware of *itself*.

The brain needs some downtime—short periods of rest so it can recharge itself. This is why meditation is invaluable—sometimes more so than rest or sleep. In sleep, the body may have stopped but the mind may still be running.

Meditation is a technique of being aware, completely present, immersed in and surrendered to one specific thing. If focused on intently, tasks such as washing dishes, brushing one's teeth, or being engaged in a creative pursuit can be treated as a form of meditation.

But what most people consider meditation is generally practiced when one is sitting or lying down in a quiet, peaceful space. It is helpful to wear loose, comfortable clothes, and for the room you are in to be dark. Some people like to listen to music that is tranquil, ambient, and repetitive while they meditate. The meditation environment should accommodate each person's needs in order to shut out all external interruptions (such as mobile phones, computers, and noisy people) so he can direct his focus inward.

Here's an example of a meditation technique.

1. Sit cross-legged on the floor, either with both legs crossed over one another or with only one leg crossed over the other. Straighten your back—this can be achieved by rolling the hips forward, allowing the lumbar vertebrae to naturally stack on top of one another and causing them to curve inward while letting the stomach gently support the back. Rest the palms of your hands on your knees or let your hands rest in your lap. Once you are seated, this posture can also be found by placing the center of focus in a point in the stomach about two inches below the navel. By gently rocking back and forth a few times, you should eventually come to rest in a comfortable position. You can also do this seated in a comfortable chair as long as your back is well supported. If your back is weak, try sitting on a pillow (some of which are designed specifically for this function), with your legs still on the floor. If sitting is too difficult, you can also lie on your back with your hands by your sides.

2. Once your posture is attained, close your eyes or keep them open slightly. If your eyes are open, you can choose a point in the room or a specific object to concentrate on while meditating.

3. Keep your breathing relaxed, easy, and even—not shallow. Some people meditate by paying attention to their breathing. Other forms of meditation include such things as chanting or repeating a mantra. The purpose of this is to distract the mind from its chatter and focus it on something that is constant, steady, and, often, repetitious. Be aware of each breath as you take it. As you follow each breath, become aware of where in the cycle the inhalation starts, where it peaks or ends, then where the exhalation starts and where it ends. You can also try to visualize your breath moving and having a shape.

4. Count ten pairs of in-and-out breaths as one cycle. After counting one cycle of ten in-and-out breaths, start over and repeat this for ten to fifteen minutes. You can set a timer to let yourself know when you are done.

5. Random thoughts may arise while meditation is taking place. There is no need to resist them; instead, simply permit them to arise, after which, you can bring yourself back to your meditation.

The mind, which usually wanders and runs wild, may become overactive while meditating because it suddenly has less control over your consciousness. It isn't used to stillness and is used to being in control. When there is any effort to still the mind, it actually begins to panic and tries to assert its primacy over consciousness by creating these random thoughts.

You can put this into perspective by considering how uncomfortable you feel when you don't have a computer or smartphone nearby, are not occupied with some task, and are completely quiet. Feels a little weird, doesn't it? Now consider your mind and objectify it as an autonomous, conscious entity that is used to constant sensory bombardment and it is suddenly being forced to be calm.

The mind can also be considered as being like a spoiled child—one that we haven't raised very well. Instead of teaching this child, we have permitted it to run wild and have its own way without instilling discipline or responsibility.

Unchecked, the mind can be willful and rebellious, but ultimately it craves the discipline and peace attainable through meditation. Like everything else, even the mind needs a break now and then. Consistently meditating once a day helps discipline the mind, helps it to unify with the body in greater harmony, and enhances concentration.

You may notice a change after a few weeks of meditating. Often, the change is noticeable immediately. It often becomes easier to concentrate on work and to interact with others. Generally, feelings of helplessness and being at the mercy of your emotions will subside.

The meditation procedure described here is not the only way to meditate—there are countless books available on the subject, as well as ample information online. I have one friend who meditates by literally thinking of nothing. He objectifies the idea of nothing as an enormous black space or a ball that fills up his consciousness completely, leaving no room for anything else, and he stays focused on that.

There has been extensive writing about meditation in daily life and how it can be applied to specific activities. The Vietnamese

Buddhist scholar Thich Nhat Hanh has written a book called *The Miracle of Mindfulness: A Manual on Meditation*, which addresses this subject in depth. There are also relaxation exercises that can provide a brief respite from an overactive mind. The following exercise is very simple and requires little preparation other than having some free time and a place to relax.

1. Make yourself comfortable, preferably lying on your back. You can play some soothing music, put a blanket on yourself—anything that will make you as relaxed as possible.
2. Start by counting backward from ten. When you reach one, you can start concentrating on your toes. Imagine releasing all of the tension that has been stored there.
3. Next, do the same thing with your feet. You can feel your feet and toes gradually relaxing as the tension and stress leave them.
4. Move to your lower legs and do the same thing. All the other parts of your body will continue to relax as you work your way through your body.
5. Continue by relaxing your knees, your thighs, your hips, and your abdomen. Don't forget your arms, hands, and fingers.
6. When you get to your face, relax each part—mouth, nose, eyes, forehead, and ears.
7. You have relaxed your entire body. It will feel completely loose and limp. Be aware of this sensation and concentrate on it while thinking of nothing else. You will feel as if you are drifting peacefully.
8. When you are ready, count backward from ten, gradually bringing your attention back to your surroundings.

When you reach one, you will be completely aware of where you are, feeling refreshed and awake.

USING YOUR BODY AS A MECHANISM TO JUDGE CREATIVE WORK

When I was little I used to listen to a variety of music, imagine instrumental parts that weren't there, and hum them. If I listened to a rock record, I'd simulate the sound of the rhythm section using my teeth as drums and constricting the muscles in my ear to emulate the resonance of the bass drum. I'd completely shut out the world and immerse myself in the feelings I got from the music I heard. I'd absorb what I listened to, atomic particle by atomic particle, and imitate its sound in my mind. I always looked for the intensity in music—something riveting and stimulating that either made me feel completely alive and connected to everything or transported me to another dimension—a different plane of existence.

That intensity translated itself into a feeling—a physical sensation. I could refer to this sensation as an endorphin rush, a feeling like my chest was opening and the front of my head was tingling, or perhaps characterize it as a feeling of complete freedom. Although it has no name or identity, it is my benchmark and I've both sought and found it in every piece of art or music that I wound up loving.

Now, when I listen to other people's work, I employ a similar methodology to the one I used when I was younger. I still rely on physical cues or sensations from inside my body to determine how I feel about the music I hear. If I'm not literally *feeling* the music I'm listening to, something is wrong.

A performer brings his entire life into a recording with him, as well as his emotional state, when he is being recorded. Because music is expressive and communicated, it isn't unreasonable that a listener should be able to discern the performer's emotional state from experiencing his performance.

If listening to music this way is unfamiliar, it may take a little time to become used to it. It simply requires patience, concentration, sensitivity to your body, and a strong awareness of what makes you feel good or bad. Gradually, you can become attuned to how your body reacts when it is in situations that are pleasurable or uncomfortable, when you are around people who make you feel good or uncomfortable, and when you are listening to music that you find either pleasing or unpleasant.

I have my own familiar set of sensory cues that inform me on a subtle level about what's happening in the world around me. For example, when I'm listening to music that is being performed without any emotion or excitement, I tend to get physically tired and will often nod out. When I feel as if a performer is losing focus, I find myself distracted by other things that are superfluous to the performance. When I'm listening to music that is being performed with enthusiasm, expression, and passion, I feel a tingling sensation in my arms, a very excited, agitated sensation as though I've had electricity shot through deep into my chest, and I can't pay attention to anything else.

Apart from building discipline and maximizing efficiency, this is one of the most important reasons that maintaining body sensitivity and awareness is so vital. Using sensory cues as a guide to determine what feels good or bad in judging creative work is far more accurate than using an arbitrary system based on personal taste or values. The body never lies when it encounters something that feels good or bad to it, whereas subjectivity is invoked when personal taste based on a thought process is the determining factor in judging creative work.

SHARED LISTENING

Chances are, most popular music artists in the Western Hemisphere don't compose music that sounds much like the music of rain-forest pygmies or Burundi drummers. But in some way all music forms are related and draw from the same roots.

Once an artist becomes aware of what to listen for and how he feels while he's listening to it, he can become more open to many different forms of music as points of reference and even inspiration. By cultivating this awareness, any artist can achieve a powerful sensory experience from music that may initially appear to be beyond his understanding.

In many cases, this is music that is made for either the purpose of religious ritual, societal utility, story-telling, or the sheer joy of making it—all of which are unfamiliar motivators to musical artists who live in a society that demands results, applauds fame, and recognizes only those who can monetize the way they spend their time.

Exposure to cultural motivators and expressions that feel alien often causes the "cognitive dissonance" we addressed earlier. This disorientation can help take an artist into realms of greater personal expression.

Apart from how alien certain ethnic and folk music may sound, one other aspect is that there isn't an arbitrary, yet strictly adhered-to criteria of perfection, unlike the mannered, polished, melismatic vocal stylings of most "composed" pop music. Folk music is often more raw, visceral, compelling, and real than other forms of music. This is because it can't be anything other than what it is.

The French have a term *jolie laide*, and it means "beautiful ugliness." This phrase pertains to people who are not classically beautiful but have unusual and, thereby, attractive features. It can be said that voices in some folk music are reminiscent of this. They do not sound pretty or processed—instead, they are often twangy, unpleasant, and harsh but they are also real and leave nothing to the imagination.

7

ARTIST MANIPULATION

There is an unspoken but prevalent feeling in the music industry that artists are valuable in name alone and serve no other possible function. This is something I encounter fairly regularly, from those poor artists being ferried aimlessly from one songwriter-producer to another in the foolhardy hopes that this will somehow "domesticate" them, to records being completed, to the tune of hundreds of thousands of dollars, only to be forever shelved because one powerful executive at the record company knows the words to that timeless chestnut, "I Don't Hear the Hit."

This type of behavior has been a constant in the music business from many years ago, when managers, producers, and notorious record company executives with ties to organized crime (like Morris Levy) would manipulate naïve artists for their own gain. These days, artists can still be manipulated, albeit in a different fashion, because the manipulation can be spun into a fairy tale in which everyone makes a ton of money and lives happily ever after. In fact, I have noticed stealthy attempts by those running the business to convince everyone else that it is not only necessary, but in the best interests of everyone involved for the artist to be thus manipulated. Why, it even benefits the artist himself, since he is unable to think for himself.

Of course, it's far easier to take advantage of people when you can objectify them instead of seeing them as human beings with pulses and thoughts and bills to pay. Business people—especially music business people—view artists as being highly emotional and unstable (since this is the way music business people often describe artists in private). Simply put, art is bad for business.

Not only is art bad for business, but one could also say that it infects those who make it—and therefore, it's akin to a disease. And, music business people believe that they have the cure for the disease called "art": keep the artist as far away from it as possible. They feel that instead of being the focal point, an artist is a troublesome pest and should be uninvolved in creative decision making, as well as any decision making that concerns him and his career.

Over the past fifty years, the music industry has gradually come to resemble a proper business with bona fide safeguards to protect naïf-like artists and educate them so they can defend themselves accordingly. All so-called safeguards notwithstanding, the recording industry is no less exploitative than it was in the good old days—in every way, and a few new ones, too.

Record companies are expert at finding loopholes in contracts—even though safeguards exist for the benefit of artists and other independent contractors who are also royalty beneficiaries, record companies are noteworthy in their ability to skirt around them. They connive artists to sign ridiculous "360 deals," wherein the artist signs away 50 percent of his touring income, 50 percent of his merchandise income, and 50 percent of his publishing. The record companies' justification is that everyone needs to profit from the artist's work—not just the artist—and merely releasing a record probably won't bring in the same kind of revenue as it would have ten years ago.

To a lot of industry types, the artist is nothing more than a cash cow, a means to an end. And when the sands of time have run out and the artist's looks are shot, when his usefulness has run its course and he has ceased to sell records, he is presented with a one-way ticket to that final stop on the fame train, the metaphorical glue factory of music—he loses his recording contract. And if an artist is one of that unfortunate multitude who has never been offered a recording contract, he winds up relegated to the subterranean depths of unsung, obscure iniquity—a veritable untouchable in the caste system of the music business.

Of course, we constantly hear about those artists who are real trouble with a capital *T*. These are the prima donnas with continent-size egos whose names are constantly being dropped on every faux-news outlet from TMZ to AOL and get attention for every asinine stunt they pull when they're not making music. These are the bad apples who spoil the idea of artistry while putting a bad light on true artists in the process. Sadly, as a result of this misconception, the stereotype of the "difficult" artist is often cast upon an individual who simply has strong feelings about his work and how it will be presented. Once upon a time, people such as these were praised for being true to their art and beliefs.

On too many pop recordings, there is an unspoken cabal between the record producer, the record company, and often, the artist's management. This relationship is proportionally more intimate between those parties, depending on how high profile the project is and how much money is involved. Sandwiched in the middle of this relationship is the artist.

These days, making a recording is easy. Virtually anyone can do it at home with a laptop. The question is, how do you infuse quality into this process? To make the best possible recording with an artist, you must strive to bring out the best in him. This will happen if you learn to respect him, and a good way to start doing this is by recognizing the humanity you both share.

Since there is less money to be made by producing records than ever before, many producers have embraced the notion of spending less time on the records they make. And, having accepted this idea as their new gospel, many producers choose to dispense with anything that might slow them down as they rush to finish what they're doing and move on to the next project. As a result, the artist's sensibilities and feelings about his work often become trivialized. Being attentive to the artist's needs takes time, and too much time costs the producer money. This point of view is one more component that has transformed recording from a once wildly creative undertaking into little more than a business transaction.

Recording used to be about falling in love with an artist's music, helping build his career, and giving him what he needed in the immediate present (and perhaps, for the future) so that he could develop and grow. Over the past thirty years, recording has become a speculative venture that revolves around two basic principles: the artist's advance money—which everyone in his periphery will take a percentage of—and the imaginary revenue that will be generated after an artist's most recent music is released.

It is ironic that the business people seem to do most of the speculating, even as the harsh realities of the industry become harsher still. One such reality concerns the elusive nature of success in any creative endeavor. Statistically, it has always been highly unlikely that any artist will succeed—artistically or financially—in music. Being a successful musician has become even more remote now that the recording industry is dying.

The reality is that it is far more likely that an artist will fail—and very badly. And if an artist is likely to fail no matter what he does, and no amount of manipulating or massaging his sound into something familiar or prefabricated will save him, why shouldn't he be permitted the dignity to fail making exactly the kind of music he wants to make? Why, in the process of failing, shouldn't he feel he has adequately represented himself and has produced something he can be proud of? What's the point in trying to make him into something he isn't, if that won't change his fate in the long run?

Failure is a great teacher of life's lessons. Exposure to failure and loss is also exposure to life's true nature and helps a person become stronger. If we allow for failure and pay attention to it, it will teach us many lessons, such as whether to stay in the ring and keep swinging or to bow out gracefully.

Why not let the artist fail doing what he loves most? Why not teach him that failure is something successful people do over and over, instead of indicating that he has one shot and then, he's finished? If he's tenacious, and perhaps lucky, someday he might actually be able to support himself doing his art. What's wrong with that? Until recently, artists were often able to build their careers precisely because they'd been permitted prior opportunities to fail and to learn from the experience.

The artist must be seen as an individual—as unique and separate and not as an extension of the producer. It is imperative that the producer get to know the artist, recognize him and take the time to respect his humanity and needs. The producer must also realize that he needs the artist as much as the artist needs him.

A record producer chooses to collaborate with an artist and to assist in making the artist's work better. Without the artist's work, the record producer has no job, no purpose, and nothing to work on. It's strange to me that such inescapable logic has become lost on so many record producers (and music business executives) over the past few decades.

An artist needs answers—he seeks a point of reference that only someone with the producer's experience can give him. A producer has choices because he is a free agent and not married to the project in exactly the same way the artist is. A producer can ignore these realities and make each record he produces exactly the same way, or he can actively contribute and make each recording a unique experience.

When a project is completed, both the artist and producer will walk away from it. However, the producer is the only one who can truly leave it behind. The artist will have to live with the results of the collaboration for the rest of his life.

If a record producer works, thinks, and acts according to his own ethics, he will always be committed to doing the right thing, without an agenda. Considering the importance of his role in the creative process, this perspective has great value.

8

WHAT IS THIS SONG ABOUT?

When working with an artist who writes her own material, I always ask her to break down and explain each song for me as thoroughly as possible. I do this for the following three reasons:

1. So the artist can talk about the song to me in her own words, and I can have her perspective on it as well as mine.
2. So the artist is put into a direct, conscious relationship with her own work—she is reminded of what the intent was behind the song when she wrote it. This may be something she never considered prior to me asking about it.
3. So I can better understand the song and get a feel for where to take it conceptually. If I have a handle on the mood of a given song, I will be better able to help musically enhance the mood and serve the artist's vision.

When I ask this of an artist, I make it clear that she is not being judged for her work or her explanation of it. I'm always conscious of maintaining a safe environment where the artist can express herself freely and speak openly without fear of being attacked, interrogated, or mocked.

I'm also aware that I'm analyzing very delicate parts of a sensitive person's consciousness. By working with the artist and then asking her to expose herself (which is a likely by-product of explaining the meaning behind her work), I'm asking a lot. Even when I assure the artist that she is safe to speak openly about her music, it often feels very foreign to have that level of trust, and she may initially hold back. As time goes on and she sees how this process can benefit her, the artist gradually becomes more comfortable about sharing and the real work can begin.

I see a song as having various layers, and I like to address them individually.

The first layer is the *text* of the song—how the lyrics read and what they project on the surface.

The second layer is the *subtext*. There are often multiple layers of subtext in a song (which can be evoked through elements such as the lyrics, melodies, and structure), and it is important for all these layers to be identified. For example, a song about love may also contain subtext that describes loss in order to provide contrast and a deeper meaning to the text. The subtext of a song may be mainly implicit.

The third layer is the song's *mood*. Mood gives a song its atmosphere, its spatial awareness and imagery. Whether it's dark, heavy, light, or sweet, I will sometimes ask the artist to provide word associations or adjectives that describe the mood she is attempting to project through her work. Some artists' music is mainly mood based and the text has no literal meaning. Here, the lyrics may serve to generate images that enhance the mood or the emotional resonance of the song.

The fourth layer pertains to the *emotion* or *feeling* of the song. The feeling of the song is the visceral sensation a listener gets from it. This is the emotional intent that the artist is projecting through the song, whether consciously or unconsciously.

It is where one experiences the living consciousness of both the song and the artist.

When the artist describes a song, I suggest that she employ word associations and describe mental images in order to break down what she intended the song to feel like. In addition to reminding the artist of what her song means to her, this helps her to experience the song vicariously from my perspective as a third party. Having these unique perspectives on her own work is both enlightening and challenging. Additionally, it helps me develop an intimate relationship with it. In this way, I can virtually "see" a song through the eyes of its creator and still be objective enough to envision how to improve it.

For the best results, I will sometimes approach the artist from a position of vulnerability, or by finding common ground between us. Generally, if the artist sees me as being open and vulnerable to her, she is often more inclined to be comfortable divulging her own feelings. One way I might do this is to ask the artist to explain her song to me as though she is speaking to a small child.

DIALOGUE REGARDING WHAT THE SONG IS REALLY ABOUT

Working with R. F., I felt that there was a certain emotional detachment in previous versions of her songs. I decided to speak in depth with her about the meaning of her material to avoid the potential for the same emotional disconnect when we recorded them.

Michael: In order for me to do the best job I can to interpret your songs musically, it helps me to get inside them. One of the best ways to do this is for you to describe to me what they mean—what you meant to say through them.

R. F.: Okay, that sounds kind of strange to me. I guess I feel uncomfortable talking about my songs. Do I have to?

Michael: No, you don't have to—it just makes it easier for me to understand them and to help you make them better.

R. F.: Well, you've heard them; can't you figure them out?

Michael: Perhaps, but I didn't write them. That means I don't have an intimate connection with them the way you do, as the writer. If I can get that insight from you, it makes it easier for me to interpret your concept into sounds and musical ideas.

R. F.: Well...I feel kind of uncomfortable doing this...

Michael: You are in control here. You can just describe to me anything about them—what comes to mind when you hear them, what you were thinking when you wrote them, what the subtext might be for you. Stuff like that. Pretend that I'm a five-year-old kid and you need to explain these things to me simply so that I'll understand them completely. Because I'm also not a very quick five-year-old. You're in control—you can tell me exactly what you want. It's like you're educating me.

R. F.: All right, but I still feel weird about this.

Michael: I understand. Just pretend I'm not all there and you have to talk down to me to help me understand your music. What is this song about? What did you feel when you wrote it? What were you trying to communicate?

R. F.: I don't know. I'm not really sure. I haven't thought about it.

Michael: We both know it came from somewhere. These lyrics mean something to you. Just pretend you're trying to explain this stuff to me because you need to. And remember, I'm a little slow. This will help you. I'll be able to get a better grasp on what the song is about and we can use that to make the song have more meaning.

R. F.: Okay, this feels really weird. Are you sure we have to do this?

Michael: I know it feels weird but it helps a lot. Just talk about the first things that come to mind when you think of this song. You can even do word associations. What's the first thing that comes to mind?

R. F.: I'm not sure.

Michael: Is this song dark, or is it light?

R. F.: I guess it's dark.

Michael: It seems kinda Gothic to me.

R. F.: Yeah, but also like an old saloon—or like a bordello.

Michael: Okay, that's good. That helps me. What else? I can feel anger in it; is it sad, too?

R. F.: Not so much; it's more spiteful. It's also about something I held onto—it still hurts but I can't let it go.

Michael: And what is that?

R. F.: It's personal—I'd rather not say.

Michael: Okay, I respect that. If you change your mind, I'll be interested to hear about it.

R. F.: It's kind of a morality play, too. I'm telling this person that he hurt me, but I actually hurt him first.

Michael: You mention God and the Devil a lot.

R. F.: Well, there's a lot in there about damnation and redemption. We're both damned for our sins, because of the choices we've made. Kind of like everyone. The human condition, basically. We're all damned for our sins, and our mortality is the proof. I guess I think everyone is going to hell.

9

DECONSTRUCTING FEEL

The term *feel* generally refers to the relationship between note values and the spaces between notes in a solo instrument performance. It also refers to the relationship between rhythm instruments, and between instruments and vocals. Feel is also referred to as "groove" or "pocket." You know it when you hear it.

In music, relationships between instruments are established by using shared points of reference. For instance, when instruments are playing together, they usually follow the same timing reference or tempo.

Once tempo is established, the relationship between instruments playing together in a group is redefined by having each instrument play different rhythmic patterns in relation to each other. Rhythmic variety among a group of instruments playing a piece of music together often makes the music sound better and more interesting. When each instrument in a group playing a piece of music plays slightly different rhythmic patterns from one another, it can be said that they are playing together *polyrhythmically*.

Tension between the instruments (how they push or pull against one another) can make polyrhythmic playing even more interesting. In order to introduce tension, instruments play together *interdependently*. I like to use the term *interdependence* because, while each instrument occupies its own rhythmic/

musical space, it also interacts with other instruments and establishes a groove. In this case, each instrument maintains its individuality and isn't entirely dependent on another, yet they all work together at performing their specific functions while creating a unified sound.

Interdependent playing is contingent on the idea that although instruments are being played together in a piece of music, they may not always land on all the downbeats they share in precisely the same way. Instead, there are very minute timing differentials between the instruments that are generally felt more than heard.

The variability of this timing differential and the ability of each performer to play with it as they wish is what determines tension and feel in music.

Feel is evident in any form of music that doesn't require all the instruments to hit every nearest downbeat simultaneously. Most music that is electronic does not have any real feel, because the downbeats and spaces between notes are always identical.

Interdependent playing has its roots in the diverse ethnic, tribal, and ritual music of many different cultures and societies. It is readily evident in African and African-derived folk music.

All music that is influenced by the legacy of African music features minute timing differentials as a distinguishing characteristic. Feel and interdependent playing can be found in black American folk music, blues, gospel music, field hollers, boogie-woogie, swing, and jazz, all of which are derived from African music. These attributes are also important aspects of other music forms that have been accepted into the mainstream of

American popular music, such as R&B, doo-wop, rock 'n' roll, soul, pop, and rock music.

Key aspects regarding the feel of an instrumental performance are note accents, note duration, and spacing between notes. The degree (and placement) of accents and the duration of notes or the spaces between notes are also signature characteristics of how specific musicians hear music and approach performance, as each one does this slightly differently.

Even though some drummers have remarkable internal time and never deviate from a click track, human beings don't play their instruments so they sound indistinguishable from machines. Frankly, I can't imagine why anyone would want to. The fact is that human performance and feel are far more interesting (and appealing to the ear) than a machined, edited human performance. Human feel in a musical performance is engaging, tense, visceral, and sexual. It is the embodiment of life force through music and identifies who the performer is.

The mechanics of feel can be illustrated by deconstructing a basic kick drum/snare drum/hi-hat pattern, wherein the kick drum is playing the odd-numbered quarter notes (beats 1 and 3 in a bar), the snare drum plays the even quarter notes (beats 2 and 4 in the bar), and the hi-hat plays eighth notes.

In order to inject a groove into our hypothetical kick/snare/hi-hat beat (in this case, at a medium tempo), we will introduce a pronounced emphasis on the downbeat of each bar (first quarter note). This accent is also characterized by a slight push. Since it is the first beat in the bar, this accent falls on the kick drum and sets up how the part will be played.

Because of the imprecise nature of human feel, ten different drummers would play this drumbeat completely differently perhaps emphasizing different parts of the groove. Imagine how a drummer such as John Bonham might play it, as opposed to Sly Dunbar, Phil Rudd, Ginger Baker, or Mick Fleetwood.

The next accent will occur either on the following half note (next bass drum hit) or on the following quarter note (next snare drum hit). The placement of the following accent can be dependent on the type of music this drumbeat is being played to.

Normally, in rock music all the quarter notes (which are played on the kick or snare) are emphasized with accents or pushes. In turn, the eighth notes (hi-hat) are also generally accented on the quarter notes and de-emphasized on the upbeats (alternating eighth notes). This creates a sense of forward motion; it also creates a back-and-forth or rocking motion. In this way, the movement of the beat becomes loose, instead of feeling robotic or stiff. The beat begins to swing.

Sex and movement figure heavily into musical rhythm, since rhythm is also an element of sex and motion. Without lateral movement in rhythm—as well as forward movement—there would be no interest in the rhythm, and it would be lifeless.

In addition to the emphasis of downbeats—and de-emphasis of specific upbeats—there is an internal timing differential between the various instruments in a drum kit.

If our hypothetical drumbeat is recorded to a click (so we have tempo reference) and analyzed as a waveform in Pro Tools, you would probably see that the instruments that are playing only quarter notes—or playing with accented pushes (kick and snare)—are playing slightly ahead of their nearest downbeats. You can see this by looking at a waveform pattern of drum hits relative to bar/beat lines.

The hi-hat, on the other hand, is not pushing, although there are accents being played on quarter-note downbeats. Instead, it winds up slightly behind the nearest downbeats. This playing behind the beat (or laying back) is further emphasized by the de-emphasized upbeat eighth notes.

If the hi-hat hits are compared to those of the kick drum—either by listening or by viewing in the Pro Tools session—there will always be an almost imperceptible timing differential or offset, a very slight *flam.*

Another way of looking at this is to consider each beat as having a front portion and a back portion. The kick and snare will wind up somewhere on the front portion of the beat, and the hi-hat will wind up on the back portion of the beat. By observing each beat as an object with dimension and fluidity, instead of a solid and unwavering reference, it is possible to play with timing and discover which instrument placement feels best, and where.

The combination of timing offsets between the kick drum, snare, and hi-hat, with the pushes on the kick and snare, creates tension and establishes feel. When a musician becomes used to playing simple beats with feel, the same approach can be applied to many other kinds of beats and rhythms.

Here is a short list of song references that are also great examples of feel:

"The Chain" —Fleetwood Mac
"Cissy Strut" —The Meters
"Let's Take It to the Stage" —Funkadelic
"Papa's Got a Brand New Bag" —James Brown
"Sunshine of Your Love" —Cream
"Whole Lotta Love" —Led Zeppelin

"Cissy Strut" has a unique drumbeat (characteristic of "second line"–style drumming) and is a great example of feel-based playing. The kick drum and snare drum are pushed and accented—each in its own way. The hi-hat lays back and reinforces tension in the drum kit.

"Whole Lotta Love" is also unique. When the drums enter after the other instruments have established themselves, the effect is stunning. Immediately, the song dynamic goes into overdrive from a 0 to a bobbing and weaving 60 inside one enormous drum fill. John Bonham is a far more brutal player than Ziggy Modeliste (the Meters) and demonstrates how feel works in a midtempo, guitar-driven rock song.

One interesting detail about this track is how tape echo was used on the drum kit to simulate a sixteenth-note tambourine groove. This trick helps accentuate the lateral aspect of the feel.

Popular music (and most ethnic or folk music) is generally presented as an interaction between a group of musicians playing instruments. A drum kit may also be perceived as a conglomeration of several instruments, all of which are interacting with one another as they interact with the other instruments in a group.

In rock music, a rhythm section usually consists of drums, bass guitar, and guitar. When identifying how these instruments interact, I feel that the relationship between the kick drum and bass guitar is a starting point. While drums can be considered the backbone of a piece of music, the bass guitar is what propels the music forward.

The bass guitar creates this sense of propulsion by playing slightly "ahead" of the drums. I often reference how far ahead the bass guitar is to where the kick drum hits land (and later, to where the guitar is played).

The following are several reasons why feel has become a less prevalent aspect in popular music since the 1980s:

1. There has been a gradual influx of electronic instruments, electronic rhythm devices, drum machines, and sequencers into popular music.

2. The advent of punk rock put less emphasis on musical skill or ability, and more on theatrics and the DIY aesthetic. Often, musicians were attempting to shun conventional styles or approaches to playing in a group. They also eschewed most rock music as a matter of course (or as a means of rebelling against established norms). In spite of this, some English punk rock bands, such as the Clash, were heavily influenced by R&B and Jamaican music. Over time, the emphasis in punk rock performance shifted to the guitar being ahead of bass and drums.

3. Click tracks had been used in recording sessions for years, and even longer in motion-picture scoring. Additionally, producers who had to deal with a new generation of musicians who were spawned in the punk era (and were comparatively unskilled) also used click tracks in order to have the musicians play in time together. Gradually, there was a greater emphasis on playing "on" with the click (as opposed to using the click as a general timing indicator).

4. There has been an influx of Pro Tools and other DAW-based recording systems that feature extensive editing capabilities. This was roughly synchronous with a general lack of emphasis on musicians being required to demonstrate proficiency on their instruments in a recording.

5. There was still an expectation for records to have a "professional" sound and appearance to them. Because recording budgets had coincidentally begun to dwindle at this time, the onus was on the record producers and technicians to pick up the slack, which they subsequently did.

As with drums, it is easy to examine the timing differential of the bass guitar against the drums—and more rigid timing references, such as gridded bar/beat lines in any DAW or electronic click track. Recording a bass guitar, playing eighth notes over our drumbeat, and taking care to play ahead of the drums, we can see where each note falls relative to the hits on the drum track.

Playing ahead of the drums can also make a piece of music seem faster and more lively than it actually is, often by 1 to 5 bpm. This translates into more excitement and lateral motion. Similar to the timing differential of the hi-hat, the bass guitar also may flam slightly against the drums—most notably the kick drum—because they are both in a similar frequency range. This flamming is not readily audible when all the instruments are playing together.

To emphasize feel, some notes in a bass guitar performance are more or less accented. Similar to the drums, the downbeat at the top of each bar will often be heavily accented, often followed by an accent on beat 3 of the bar, which is also where the kick drum is pushing.

In order to stay ahead of the drums and still work metrically with them, the bass guitar phrasing must change slightly. This is helpful when playing eighth notes, as they can be transformed from feeling stiff to feeling fluid and having "swing."

The bass guitar performance must "compress" some of its phrases—or alter note durations—in order to play with the drums. Similar to how the hi-hat played eighth notes, the bass guitar will ideally emphasize the quarter-note downbeats and de-emphasize the upbeat eighth notes.

The following songs are a few noteworthy examples of interdependent playing with respect to bass guitar:

"Dreams" —Fleetwood Mac
"Give It Up or Turnit a Loose" —James Brown
"Helter Skelter" —The Beatles
"Ramble On" —Led Zeppelin
"Rock and Roll" —Led Zeppelin
"Sympathy for the Devil" —The Rolling Stones

"Rock and Roll," by Led Zeppelin, is one of my favorite examples of interdependent bass and drums. This is because the rhythm section is essentially nothing more than an exciting drumbeat accompanied by a bunch of eighth notes played on the bass guitar. Of course, where Led Zeppelin is concerned, it's as much in the "how" as it is in the "what."

Let's imagine this song performed by a contemporary band and surgically edited in a digital audio workstation (DAW). Without the arrogant sexy swagger, without the feel, it would become stiff and unexciting—nothing more than a dull three-chord jam with goofy lyrics. However, primarily because of how the rhythm section plays together, the song is vital, visceral, and thrilling. They provide the vocalist with all the room he needs. The bass and drums cause the track to bounce—they generate a steady pulse with pushes on the quarter notes. In spite of this, one can also feel the rush of eighth notes and a slight emphasis on the backbeats.

There is an up-and-down, lateral, front-to-back motion occurring, which I can best describe as being 3-D. The drums push hard against the tempo of the song, and the bass pushes even harder against the tempo and against the drums. The extreme tension created by the interplay of these two instruments turns this song into an adrenaline rush—and one of the most exciting pieces in the rock music lexicon.

"Helter Skelter," by the Beatles, is an even more extreme example of interdependent playing between bass and drums. One of the amazing things about this song is how far ahead the bass is in relation to the drums. It becomes even more obvious when listening in headphones (the bass and drums are hard-panned apart). Nearly every shared hit winds up being a flam.

Because the bass is rushing, the illusion is created that the song is considerably faster than it actually is. This also creates much more space between the bass and drums, more swing in the track, and a greater pocket for the other instruments to work with. The feel created by the bass and drums is so extreme that it practically veers into triplets. Also interesting—John Lennon was the bassist on this track.

The fact is that no one has ever made an interesting rhythm track in which the bass guitar played consistently on time and on the exact same half of the downbeats as the drums.

Guitar is the final piece in the rhythm section. Since the late 1970s to early 1980s, the guitar gradually progressed to being played farthest ahead of the other instruments in the rhythm section. The guitar is also the loudest rhythm section instrument in recent rock recordings.

By referencing music forms that are descended from African music, we get a different idea of placement. In swing or big-band music, most instruments in the alto to soprano range tend to be played far behind the closest relative downbeats. The same is true in blues, R&B, and soul. You can follow the musical lineage from black music forms to rock music, which has relied (sometimes exclusively) on electric guitar as a signature sound. Ideally, in rock music, the guitar will "lay back" or play behind the bass and drums. Guitar placement is similar to that of the hi-hat.

This approach to guitar playing creates its own auditory illusion. For years, it has been assumed by listeners that drummers such as John Bonham were playing behind the beat (or laying back). For many years after this, drummers attempted to emulate what they thought they were hearing by playing behind the beat. Unfortunately, this approach to drumming tends to make a piece of music drag. Drummers of Bonham's era generally didn't lay back at all. It wasn't the drums people heard laying back—it was actually the placement of the guitar relative to everything else in the mix.

Other elements that affect timing relationships between instruments are their volume relative to each other in a mix, and their placement in the stereo field. A louder sound tends to be perceived as being faster by a very small increment of time, but enough to affect the feel of the band. When the guitar plays behind the beat (and in opposition to the drums and bass, which are pushing ahead of the beat), the tension that existed between the bass and drums is exponentially increased. Each instrument occupies its own space, yet each instrument interacts with each of the others. Each instrument can be subtracted from the ensemble of all the instruments playing together, be heard on its own, and still have its own unique character. The guitar will need to alter its phrasing (similar to how the bass guitar does, but in a different relationship to downbeats) in order to maintain its tension between the bass and drums. In a pattern, some notes or chords will be emphasized, some de-emphasized.

When finding the right pocket for a guitarist, I will often ask him to listen to the hi-hat or ride cymbal (assuming that it's being played behind the beat) and to place himself in that same general relationship with the rest of the band. Once he has that placement locked in, I'll ask him to focus on the backbeat. This tends to draw his focus away from the odd beats in the bar and causes him to naturally lay his part back even more, creating greater space and dramatic tension between the guitar and the other instruments.

When a rhythm section interacts this way, an overall timing differential occurs relative to the nearest downbeat (or grid line, in a DAW). This range can be roughly 5 to 10 milliseconds on either the front or back portion of the beat, depending on the instrument. The range of this timing differential creates enough room for a vocal or solo instrument to play with phrasing, timing, and so on. The following are some good references for this style of playing:

"Getting Better" —The Beatles
"Give It Up or Turnit a Loose" —James Brown
"Good Times Bad Times" —Led Zeppelin
"Helter Skelter" —The Beatles
"Hoochie Coochie Man" —Muddy Waters
"Let's Take It to the Stage" —Funkadelic
"Purple Haze" —Jimi Hendrix
"Since I've Been Loving You" —Led Zeppelin

"Give It Up..." is a perfect example of multiple instrument interaction. This is particularly noteworthy at the percussion breakdown, which occurs at about 4:25 into the song and allows the band to stop playing and then to gradually be reintroduced.

First, the drums reenter, followed by the bass guitar, which redefines and enhances the drums. Two bars later, the first guitarist begins to play, followed by the second guitarist one and a half bars later. By the time the second guitar comes in, the groove becomes a song. It has been fleshed out harmonically, and another degree of feel or interdependent playing has been established.

"Purple Haze" is yet another example of great interdependent band playing, in addition to brilliant guitar work. The band has a more flowing style—less R&B and more jazzy—but Jimi Hendrix's background is in R&B, soul, and blues. This is evident in his playing, which is a seamless combination of rhythm and lead. All of his phrasing is consistently behind the beat and this is clearly how he feels it. This approach enhances the lateral motion of a rock song, making it swing even more and infusing it with sex.

The following is a general reference of timing differentials regarding instrument downbeats (as compared to the closest relative downbeat). These times are in milliseconds and can be even greater in some cases, depending on the player or the style of music:

Kick drum	ahead 3 to 7 milliseconds
Snare drum	ahead 3 to 7 milliseconds
Hi-hat	behind 3 to 5 milliseconds
Bass guitar	ahead 3 to 10 milliseconds
Guitar	behind 3 to 7 milliseconds

10

THE PHYSIOLOGY
OF FEEL

In my mind, the downbeat is not an absolute reality. If nothing in life is truly absolute, then anything is possible. Even science is disproved and rewritten on a daily basis. For example, we still have no idea exactly how our brains work, exactly when life began on this planet, whether there are multiple dimensions, or how many of them there might be. Because we're in a constant state of discovery, our collective consciousness is in a constant state of flux.

In music, we use points of reference so that everyone knows where they are when they're playing a song. These points of reference are like landmarks, and they pertain to such elements as tempo, rhythm, key, and pitch. These landmarks are generally accepted as being die-hard and solid. Absolute.

But music is also fluid, rhythm is fluid, and landmarks aren't always accurate. And, as I've come to find, if musicians are playing a piece of music together, the downbeats aren't always absolute. And if you really think about it, how can they be? Why should they be? If a bunch of musicians playing together are determining as a group where their downbeats are going to land, isn't it possible that there's going to be pushing and pulling? Tension? Polyrhythms? Flams?

One of my favorite examples of this is Arturo Toscanini's interpretation of the second movement of Beethoven's Symphony no. 9, with the NBC Symphony Orchestra. This piece is in a superfast 3/4 time, incorporates a relentless barrage of quarter notes, and, if performed to the letter, can be very stiff. However, Toscanini's interpretation of this movement is marvelous. It breathes and moves, and it never drags. Pound for pound, it's my favorite version of this work precisely because it's so fluid and loose. The orchestra is playing the eighth notes as a unit, but it never feels stiff.

By comparison, a version of the same symphony conducted by Herbert Von Karajan (who, by the way, is another one of my favorite conductors) is completely different. Von Karajan is all about accuracy and, when he conducts, every eighth note is played with machine-like precision, as though the entire orchestra were terrified of accidentally upsetting the maestro. As a result, I feel that this version is far tighter, and therefore, less interesting. To my ears, Von Karajan had the orchestra focusing on the eighth notes, instead of concentrating on getting inside Beethoven's music.

If musicians are playing interdependently, there's little chance that everyone is going to find the absolute same place on the downbeat every time they play something. Instead, there will be an expanded sense of the downbeat—you'll be aware of the front part of the beat, the back part of the beat, and notes played far off the beat in either direction—in some cases, way off. In spite of this, it will always sound—and feel—like music.

Each musician in a group serves a defined function by approaching the performance from a different perspective. It's this human element that adds exciting tension to music and makes it interesting.

DIALOGUE REGARDING FEEL AND DOWNBEATS

In the process of recording guitar tracks with A. Z., I wanted him to pay more attention to the rhythm section so he could find his own groove.

Michael: Okay, so I want you to listen to the placement of the bass and drums. How are they sitting to you?

A. Z.: They feel great.

Michael: Good. Now, can you hear the relationship between them? What's happening there?

A. Z.: Well, the bass sounds way ahead of the drums. The drums aren't laying back because I know they were ahead of me when we tracked this. They feel like they're laying back, though. It's crazy. It sounds great.

Michael: And you feel tension, right?

A. Z.: Definitely. Tension. The bass and drums are creating tension.

Michael: Is it disturbing tension, or is it exciting tension?

A. Z.: Oh, definitely exciting. So exciting.

Michael: Okay, good. Now, it's time to put the guitar in. Let's run this song and you can play with it.

A. Z.: Okay.

[*Song plays; A. Z. plays along and we record him. We listen back.*]

Michael: A few things. First of all, we need even more excitement. That won't happen if you try to play in the same space as the bass and drums. I realize this may seem a bit counterintuitive at first, but I want you to lay back more.

A. Z.: I have a tendency to play ahead of everyone else.

Michael: Yes, and this interferes with the feel that the bass and drums have set up. In fact, if you listen, you can hear that it makes the song drag if you play in the same space with the bass and drums.

A. Z.: So, more laid back?

Michael: Yes, more. As much as possible.

[*We record again. We play the song back.*]

Michael: That's better, but still not quite it. Listen to where everyone else's downbeats are. Avoid hitting with their down beats. Establish your own. Remember how the drummer played the hi-hat a little behind his kick and snare, right? It created internal tension in the drums and made the song move differently—with more good tension.

A. Z.: Yes.

Michael: Okay, where the hi-hat is falling is roughly where you want to fall, too. But we perceive the primary downbeats of the drums and bass based on where the kick, bass, and snare fall. Every single one of those instruments is falling in a slightly different place. Listen.

[*We play back the drums and bass only.*]

So, now let's solo the kick, snare, and bass guitar.

[*These tracks are soloed; there is obvious flamming going on between all the instruments.*]

Michael: You hear that, right?

A. Z.: [*Shakes his head in disbelief.*] That's crazy. Wow.

Michael: When we put it under the microscope, you can hear that these instruments are consistently flamming. They're not bad flams and you can't hear them when there are other instruments in the mix, but there are definite differences in timing. You can hear that same type of instrument relationship in the R&B music we were listening to before. The point is that none of these instruments is really falling on the exact same downbeats. How can they if they're flamming? They're also playing their rhythms with different feels. It all works together to create a unique tension.

A. Z.: I totally hear it now. I think I hear it on every record I really love, too.

Michael: Same kind of tension in African music. The downbeats are relative—they're not absolute. Try to use that awareness when you play, and position your guitar where you want it to sit in the song—where it feels best. Try to visualize the downbeats and fit your guitar in between them. Don't let your notes fall in the same spot, or where you perceive everyone else's downbeats. You're trying to support everyone else—what they've played. You're also trying to play with everyone, but you're trying to dominate it, to take it over. It'll be harder to express yourself, or to be dominant, if you're playing in the same space as the bass and drums. You're hiding behind them—agreeing with them. The whole point of this is these instruments are successive layers of information. Each layer creates a new dimension, a new deeper way of expressing the music. You're working with the other instruments when you put your layer on top of them, but you're also taking charge and creating good tension by stating, "Okay, now I'm running this show." It makes the impact of the rhythm deeper.

[*Pause.*]

Okay, you're looking confused. That's because this goes against logic. You can't use your brain to figure it out. You have to feel it. You actually feel it. In your body. Right here.

[*Smacks his chest. Pause.*]

Because there's more depth to everything. There's a lateral motion as well as a front-to-back motion. You get a deepened sense of spatial engagement.

A. Z.: Uhhhhh... What do you mean?

Michael: You *physically* feel the pulse. You feel it as a sensory experience, and it actually makes your body move with it. It just deepens the awareness of the movement in the music. You can take a basic kick/snare drum pattern and see how a thousand drummers will play it differently, because each drummer's approach to the part is completely unique.

A. Z.: Wow, I've never thought about it like that before. It seems so foreign, but it makes complete sense. I have to unlearn how much I play to clicks all the time. When we do sessions, everyone listens and records to the same click, but no one listens or records to each other. When I worked with the Jamaican and Afro-Cuban musicians, it was all about feel and groove. I learned a lot from that experience that I've unlearned by doing sessions, and now I have to learn it all again. But in a different way.

Michael: Yes, but again, as much talking as we're doing, this isn't an intellectual concept. It's something you feel, and the only way you're going to feel it is by doing it over and over until you've established with certainty how and where the feeling is inside you. Be sensitive to yourself while you're playing and try to find the feeling.

11

DRUMS AND DRUMMERS

When drums are played with feel, they are no longer simply a means of marking time—they become a rhythmic point of reference, redefine the relationships between the other instruments, and create space in a piece of music. They transform a piece of music from a static, one-dimensional creation into a living, breathing entity. The drum performance can be appreciated as an individual expression of the drummer, not simply as a functional element in a song.

I have never felt that a drummer was great simply because he was precise or could play in perfect time, dead on with a click track. The greatest drummers express utter confidence in their ability to speak through their instrument. When you listen to a drummer who plays expressively and with feel, it is obvious that even though her tempo may be solid, certain parts of her performance may actually flam with a click.

In the past, great drummers were highly esteemed because of how different from one another their approach to performing was. Each drummer had a signature style, and using a specific drummer would set the tone for the recording he played on. The way these performers hit their drums, the tone they got, their feel, and how they interacted with other musicians on a recording are all factors that made their work outstanding. Imagine how different the Rolling Stones would have sounded if Charlie Watts had been replaced by Keith Moon or Carl Palmer.

Great drumming is about a lot more than guys who hit things for a living.

By comparison, many current recordings represent drummers as being functional, interchangeable components and largely, anonymous. They are neither required, nor even hired to stand out and participate expressively on recordings. They are used to serve a specific function: to mark time, to play a part solidly—they are expected to not deviate from a click at all and to fill space, and that's all.

In present day recording, drummers usually record their performance to a click track that is gridded in a DAW, after which, the performance is edited as tightly to the nearest sixteenth notes as physically possible. At some point, the recorded drums are generally replaced with samples.

In a sense, a heavily digitally edited recording of an instrument that a person played creates a weird amalgam. Instead of getting an actual performance, you wind up with kind of a cyborg. Not quite machine, not quite human, but often possessing the worst traits of both. Whatever you want to call it, there's generally something about it that doesn't feel quite right.

There's a degree of irony that recordings of instruments played by people are treated in such a sterile, utile manner. Drums, for example, are generally approached with the emphasis on being as machine-like and precise as possible, and then they are edited through the use of other machines so as to be even more machine-like.

It's not unusual for edited or programmed drums to get used on a pop record or on an electronic record. However, it seems kind of odd to program drums in the same way for a rock record. Aren't programmed drums—no matter how loud and punchy they are—the complete polar opposite of the rock aesthetic? Of course, there are recordings such as *Pyromania* or *Hysteria* by Def Leppard; however, they were high concept and no one makes records like that anymore. From what I understand, Mutt Lange, who produced those records, had a very specific vision in mind when he made them. As my friend the late Mike Shipley told me about making those records, "Mutt would always say, 'I don't want rock and roll, I want Star Wars!'"

Putting this into perspective, music is a highly refined mode of communication between humans and a means of transmitting their emotional states. If you're editing a performance, you're basically altering its makeup, its DNA—in this case, its ability to communicate clearly. With this in mind, I find it kind of hard to comprehend how people who make countless records with heavily edited drums, vocals, and other instrumentation never stop to consider how doing so may interfere with that essential aspect of music. In a sense, heavily editing pop music is a bit like genetically modifying food—you do it because theoretically the change should make it better (whatever that means to you), but when it's finished, you're not quite sure if you haven't made it worse.

I'm not suggesting we toss the editing software out the window just because it's an offense to God and nature. It exists and it can be helpful, where and when absolutely necessary. However, I do have an issue with the concept of depending on technology too much instead of encouraging musicians to do their job.

I also happen to feel that music is at its best when it is brimming with personality, and that it communicates and imparts far less when it is edited into absolute linear perfection, because its intrinsic personality is lost in the process. Human beings are neither linear nor perfect. We have rough edges and imperfections and we like encountering them in our art. They remind us of who we really are.

I recently had to select a drummer for a recording and wound up sorting through reams of YouTube clips. After viewing several videos, I realized I wasn't looking at a group of varied individuals with their own unique playing styles; rather, I was seeing about a dozen shades of gray.

None of these musicians was able to demonstrate a signature style or how he stood out from the gargantuan crowd of other drummers. Instead, they were all demonstrating their ability to blend in. They were showing how anonymous and inoffensive they could be. They all demonstrated the steadiness of their time, how loudly they could play, and how precise their technique was.

It made me sad to see a bunch of talented, desperate musicians vying for who was the most generic and the least unique. They all hit the mark—flawlessly.

One drummer had posted a clip of himself playing a Led Zeppelin song with his band. I can safely say that he had more precision in one of his fingernail clippings than John Bonham had throughout the course of his entire life. This drummer was an animal—rock-solid, all over the drum kit, blisteringly loud, and he never wavered. Not for an instant. His time was spot-on and letter-perfect; every hit was consistent, and I doubt a sampler could have triggered samples more accurately. His video was so painfully boring that I had to stop it after about twenty seconds.

Please, dear reader—stop reading this very instant and listen without delay to John Bonham's drumming on any random piece of music in the Led Zeppelin lexicon. I beseech thee—just do this thing and pay attention to nothing but Bonham. Listen and then return to these words immediately after.

Now, if you have just finished listening to the drums on the Led Zeppelin song of your choosing, you probably noticed (apart from his sheer magnificence) that Bonham plays consistently but he doesn't always play consistently in time. His tempo appears fine but if you put it against a click, you'll find he is fluctuating—sometimes wildly.

He speeds up, slows down—and from one perspective, it could be seen as a mess. So why, instead of being known as a sloppy drummer, is John Bonham lavished with legendary status and revered as the veritable god of rock drumming?

The answer is simple. Bonham was a true artist. I'll go so far as to state that he was genetically engineered to express himself immaculately, without restraint, and he spoke both loud and proud through his drums. He was utterly flamboyant—flashy, loud, aggressive, and seething with testosterone. He transmitted everything he was—every infinitesimal molecule—through his drumming. In so many ways, he was the antithesis of nearly everything that modern drummers appear to have become.

And even though it is still the dream of so many drummers to sound just like John Bonham, to tread the same hallowed ground Bonham trod, I doubt that Bonham would last five minutes on a modern recording session. He would be off the grid, off time, unruly, unmanageable, unapologetic. Unique. Himself.

These days, the average drummer is an ambassador of a new age of performing. Through his drumming, he plaintively tells the sad tale of how the human element has all but vanished from music and musical performance. He eschews personal expression and does either what he's told or what he assumes is expected of him. And he does it all with machine-like precision.

The drummer who plays with feel is a different animal. She can keep time, but her focus, first and foremost, is to express herself without reservation and to command the music she is playing. She owns her performance and she owns the track she is playing on.

She doesn't play drums in her specific way to please anyone or make anyone else's job in a recording studio easier. She plays drums because she has to. When you hire her for a recording, you're not getting someone to keep time and fill space—you're getting someone who gives you several minutes of her very existence.

There may be variances in her playing. Those differences could be major or minor, depending on the situation and on what the producer or engineer or artist's idea of perfect happens to be. If the drummer is playing with a click track, there may be audible flams when the click is monitored with the drum track. Many years ago, I worked with Tony Thompson (Chic's drummer, and no stranger to playing with clicks) on a recording where he played to a Roland TR808 drum machine. I couldn't help but notice that he was constantly flamming with the TR808, but his performance sounded so good, it didn't matter. He was Tony Thompson, for heaven's sake.

Another time, I was invited into someone else's session while they were playing back a drum track that Jim Keltner (who, for over fifty years, has been one of the most legendary and best-loved session drummers) had just put down. The drums lurched to and fro, the tempo shifted wildly, and Tony Berg, who was producing the track beamed with delight because it sounded so wonderful. Do you think that drum track got edited?

In spite of any variances in tempo, a drummer who plays with feel will always maintain a steady groove. She locks into that groove like the jaws of a pit bull lock up and she never deviates.

Now, consider how drums and rhythm fit into a piece of music. What is the purpose of the rhythm? What is the purpose of having drums on a recording? What does it all mean to you? Listen to different types of music. Listen to drums first, then let the other instruments gradually seep into your field of awareness. Putting the compositions and any personal preferences aside, concentrate only on the instrumental performances. Do you notice a difference between the performances in these pieces of music? If so, what is it? What kind of emotional reaction do you experience from listening to these recordings? What role did each instrument play in the way you felt? How does the drum performance in each song make you feel? How do the instruments performing together make you feel? What do you think they're trying to tell you? Does this inspire you to make your own musical statement?

What is your own groove, your own way of interpreting tempo, rhythm, and music? Listen to drumbeats, listen to how the patterns occur, listen to where each hit falls, listen to the spaces in between. Where do you fit in?

Do you play your instrument with conviction, emotion, and expression, or with conformity and resignation? Do you play as a means of expressing yourself, or to pacify other people and give them what you think they want? The deeper your commitment to what you do, the more you are able to express yourself, and the more energy will flow through your work—all of which will be communicated directly to everyone who encounters it. Ultimately, the power of music as a communicative medium comes down to two people: the performer and the listener.

12

SOME GUIDELINES FOR VOCALISTS

O f all instruments, the human voice is the only one that is generated entirely from within the human body. This is one reason that vocals and singing connect with people. The voice is the most personal instrument of all.

Everyone has a voice. Everyone can open their mouths and make a sound come out. It's a thoroughly primal experience, and yet it has been refined over thousands of years of human development. It's possible that protohumans were beating on logs before they began to sing, but it was probably never as meaningful as the first time someone raised his voice in a song of fear, sorrow, joy, or reverence.

Most liturgical music is vocal because singing is clearly the most direct route to communication with the Divine. When people listen to music, they invariably focus in the vocal first, and everything else—no matter how wonderful it might be—is experienced as an afterthought.

When you open your mouth to sing, you aren't always thinking about it, but you are instantly aware of what you are doing. As you sing, your voice creates a feedback system—the sound comes out of your body, you simultaneously feel your own emotion from the act of singing and the sensation you get from hearing your own voice. Perhaps, this is one reason so many extraordinarily untalented people go on shows like *American Idol* (apart from wanting to be seen on TV)—they experience this wonderful emotion in themselves whenever they sing, and because they feel it so deeply, they exhibit themselves with reckless abandon under the delusion that others are sharing the same experience.

When you watch a great artist sing, you are experiencing their innermost self. From Nina Simone to Aretha Franklin to Frank Sinatra, watch their faces as they are performing and you can actually see them become possessed by the song and by the act of singing. Ideally, singing is an expression of one's true self and not a mechanical recitation of a melody with words attached.

When a person is *truly* expressing himself through singing, he is also incapable of lying—although he may be singing about a fictional event or about nothing, he is communicating *exactly* who he is to the listener via his performance. The listener, in turn, experiences this truthfulness. Even if he is unaware of what is happening, he can still feel in his own viscera what the singer is feeling.

It is also easier (and much less effort) for a singer to not express himself, and instead, have his vocal performance be edited and tuned. This means he can not only avoid any emotional exertion, but he can also avoid sharing with us who he really is. When the emotional component is lost from a vocalist's performance, listeners eventually respond by tuning him out and ceasing to support him.

Singers grow artistically by listening to other singers. It is essential for a vocalist to listen to other singers perform, and to experience how these other singers express their emotions, and are totally connected to their true selves.

Mental imagery is a helpful tool to flesh out and give substance to the emotion in a song. But what images does the singer use to help him find his way into the song? And how do they make him feel? When he immerses himself in these images (and the attendant feeling that accompanies them), what happens? Do these images enhance his feeling for the song, or have they recontextualized it? What happens when he empties his mind of everything but these images and the feelings they inspire, and sings?

A comfortable, relaxed working atmosphere or environment can help to help draw the emotion out of a singer and get him deeper into his performance. An environment that evokes a strong mood, or creates an atmosphere of cognitive dissonance (and perhaps distorts the singer's perception of reality), can also be helpful—anything that takes the vocalist out of his headspace and into his body space is useful and worthwhile.

One of the most valuable things that a vocalist can learn is how to pace himself instead of pushing too hard physically, mentally, or emotionally (unless doing so absolutely guarantees optimal results, or the vocalist consciously chooses doing this for a specific reason). The vocalist is better off working within his physical range and testing himself comfortably and without damaging himself, while constantly exploring his own boundaries (technically or otherwise).

Since the voice comes from the body, it is important for the vocalist to become familiar with how his body is feeling. This means listening to, and taking cues from, his body as a barometer to establish a baseline of where the vocalist is from day to day, and moment to moment. He must not only be attentive to how he feels, he must also be attentive to how his voice sounds and if it has changed from his established baseline. The best way for the vocalist to do this is by being attentive, stopping during the day to breathe in and out every so often and return himself to his body. Sometimes, silence is golden. Meditation and light physical exercise are also helpful in developing and maintaining this baseline awareness.

Exercise within your comfort range and try to avoid extreme physical workouts, as they will weaken the body for singing. I have encountered many vocalists who, prior to a recording session, exercised well past their own physical capacity for exertion. They would then get in front of a microphone and be completely confounded when the sound of their voice resembled the hissing noise made by trying to get shaving cream out of a pressurized shaving cream dispenser that was empty.

Physical activity keeps your focus on the sensory awareness in your body, which is the optimum place to be when you are singing. It also trains you to think less and to feel more.

Always remember, as a vocalist you are *communicating*. You are sharing something very special from deep inside of yourself. The extent to which you can make your performance compelling will largely be determined by how capable you are at communicating your feelings. Once again, this is not a cerebral process and cannot be thought out, intellectualized, or even properly explained. It can only be felt and experienced.

Finding emotional depth in lyrics can become an exercise in mindfulness. Try to examine carefully what you are saying before you sing or speak. Consider your words. Feel the weight of them, and where they originate from inside of you prior to speaking. Find your intent through this exercise and remain focused on it. When you are about to sing, this will help you locate that place of mindfulness within.

Some people tend to become very warm or even overheated while singing—singing can be taxing physically, mentally, and emotionally. If you are tired after singing, you have probably done your job well. If you are exhausted, you may have tapped yourself out physically and pushed your adrenals, too. Apart from emotional exertion, vocal performance is also a cardiovascular activity that requires physical endurance, the extensive usage of specific muscle groups, and other aspects of physiology.

For these and other reasons, it is essential for a vocalist to be aware of how she feels and what her rate of burnout is. It can be helpful to think of preparing for a vocal performance in a way that is similar to how a professional athlete might train for the Olympics.

AND A FEW MORE GUIDELINES FOR THE VOCALIST

As stated in the previous section, the voice is a very delicate instrument—kind of a juncture between the rest of the body, the emotions, and the outside world. Here are some additional thoughts that are relevant to its care and maintenance.

WHEN TO TAKE A BREAK

Be mindful of when you have to stop singing (or doing anything else). It may be helpful to stop singing when

- You are becoming frustrated with performing, with other people, or anything else.
- You are becoming increasingly distracted by anything other than what you are doing.
- The top end (or air) has left your voice.
- You are feeling fatigued.
- Your voice is becoming hoarse or husky.

- You are losing control of your voice.
- You (your voice, body, mind, or emotions) are in any kind of pain or physical distress.
- You need food.
- You need liquids.
- You are hung over and you feel like you were run over by a Mack truck.

In order to be properly employed, the voice requires both strength and stamina. Feed it, exercise it (in moderation and relative to individual tolerance), lubricate and maintain it. Drink warm (not hot) decaffeinated tea. Panda black licorice can be a good lubricant for the throat, although this is not recommended if you have any issues with your sugar intake.

SUBSTANCES THAT VOCALISTS SHOULD AVOID

During the general time period in which you are singing, it is best to avoid consumption of the following:

- Caffeine (acids stimulate reflux and can burn vocal cords)
- Nicotine (be careful about quitting immediately prior to singing, as this can fatigue the body)
- Alcohol (stimulates reflux, which can burn vocal cords; beer and wine are extremely acidic)
- Chocolate (oxalic acid stimulates reflux, which can burn vocal cords)
- Any type of recreational drug (fatigues the body)
- Prescription drugs (fatigue the body)
- Any kind of sugar (wears down the body and depletes adrenaline)

- Dairy (causes phlegm to build up on the throat and vocal cords)
- Fruit (occasionally, the acid in fruit can hurt vocal cords)
- Spicy foods (acid can stimulate reflux and burn vocal cords)

SOME MISCELLANEOUS DETAILS FOR VOCALISTS

- Try to sing conversationally, as though you are speaking directly to someone.
- Brighten the tone of your vocal by raising your upper lip (smile). This often introduces more air into the vocal tone.
- Imagine a tube leading from the diaphragm up into the head. Push air up this tube from the diaphragm in order to sing with a bit more power.
- Become aware of phrasing as an element in musical performance. Listen to how other vocalists phrase. Listen to how other instruments are phrased when played. After thinking about this, how would you incorporate a different approach to phrasing into how you sing?
- While performing, stay focused and be present. If the mind wanders, bring it back to the act of singing. Singing can be considered a form of meditation, so be mindful of your performance.

DIALOGUE REGARDING VOCAL WORK

While making a record with M. C. and his band, M. C. was having trouble with his vocals. He was also uncomfortable with having me in the studio while he worked (which is natural for some vocalists), so I left him to record vocals with our engineer and checked up on him daily. I've just played back his latest vocal performance.

Michael: So, let's talk about what's going on here.

M. C.: Yeah, I know.

Michael: Really? What do you know?

M. C.: It's not good enough, right? I'm kinda hitting it, but not really.

Michael: Yeah, that's what's going on.

M. C.: Man, I'm so fucking frustrated right now. This feels like it's been going on for months and I've got a few lines. Not even one finished song.

Michael: Well, it has been going on for months. And we're getting the same results nearly every day. So, if we're getting the same results and we don't like those results, it makes sense that we might consider changing a few things we're doing so we can also change our results, right?

M. C.: I don't know, man. I guess so.

Michael: Look, we talked about this in the beginning. You wanted a record that was as good as it could possibly be. That's what we talked about doing. This is how it gets done. No one is happy with the progress we're making, but if you want a great record you have to put yourself into it. You know?

M. C.: Ugghhhh.

Michael: We both know you can do this. You have a great voice—that's not the issue. The issue is, are you going to be disciplined enough so you can get through this process? You know what you have to do. We've spoken about it. *[Pause.]* So, you got drunk this weekend, right?

M. C.: No, man. How the fuck can you tell that?

Michael: Well, did you?

M. C.: *[Pause. Sighs.]* Yes. I got drunk.

Michael: I know this because when you drink, your voice thins out and the air goes out of it within a half take. You lose your upper range, your high end, all your control; you get wobbly. You sound tired and hoarse. It isn't hard to tell. You got drunk on the weekend. You were hung over and got no sleep. You look tired, too. Are you eating anything to keep yourself replenished? Other than greasy junk food?

M. C.: Noooo...Shit.

Michael: You know that when you do this, you generally need about a week to recuperate until you're back to normal. That's how it is for most people. You're not Superman—your body can only take so much.

M. C.: I know, I know.

Michael: Okay, so this is really simple. You and me and your band—we're all on the same page. We want to make a great record. So far, it is that—a great record. We committed to do this, but we won't have that if the vocals—your vocals—aren't great, too. Right now, we're bottlenecking around your performance. We have to do better.

M. C.: Oh, man...Come on. I can't live like this.

Michael: It's either that or we start keeping the vocals you've done and cobbling vocal takes together. We can edit them and tune them. Like Britney Spears or Hoobastank. Is that what you want?

M. C.: No, I don't. I really don't want that.

Michael: You just heard this last vocal. Do you think it's good? Do you think it represents you at your best? Do you want that vocal on your record as a representation of you—something that you and the rest of the world will be hearing for as long as the record exists? Look, it isn't easy talking to you like I'm your parent. But I can't tell you what to do. I'm not your mom. It's your call.

M. C.: No. It sucks. I heard it. I sound like ass.

Michael: Yeah, but you know you don't have to sound like ass. Just hang in there a bit longer, hold off from the drinking and the hangovers. Eat better and get some rest. Exercise, too—cardio—don't kill yourself. All this stuff works. You'll get better vocals like this. You'll see.

M. C.: Okay, I'll try.

Michael: Think how happy you'll feel at the end of the recording. You'll be able to reward yourself with a week of nonstop drinking and the worst hangover you've ever had if that's what you really want. But by then, it won't affect your vocals. You'll have something to look forward to when you're done.

M. C.: Yeah, sure. Very funny.

13

THE SIGNIFICANCE OF
CREATIVE WORK

There is a line in the Bhagavad Gita that states, "Better to do one's own duty imperfectly than to do another man's well." To me, this statement addresses and resolves one of the greatest dilemmas facing creativity in a few brief words.

What does this statement mean to you? Take a moment and let the words sink in—we'll come back to them.

Here's another question—what do you feel is the most significant commodity in the domain of creative work? This is an interesting question and, oddly, I've never heard it asked by anyone in any creative field. Perhaps people don't take the subject seriously enough, have taken it for granted far too long, or have simply never considered it.

What gives creative work its meaning? If you play an instrument, is it great technique? Is it the ability to dance while you lip-sync? Is it the ability to solve problems and multitask with great ease? What about discipline and perseverance? Does it pertain to Malcolm Gladwell's concept of applying ten thousand hours of dedication to your chosen endeavor? Is it raw, naked talent, or is it raw, naked ambition?

The answer is, it's none of these things, although they certainly don't hurt. The most valuable commodity in the domain of creative work is also the most readily available. It is the most common, because it exists in every single person on the face of this earth and yet, in its distilled form, is the thing that flows unhindered from the greatest of artists. It unites people and speaks to them on the deepest possible level. This commodity is the resource known as *expression.*

In art, creative work is all about an artist's ability to be expressive. The more expressive an artist is, the more profound, effective, and palpable his message is. The greater the extent to which his message can be understood, the more he can reach out and communicate with other people.

This requires an artist to be as transparent and as genuine as he is capable. Like a tribal shaman, an artist is a kind of conduit that allows energies and consciousness from outside himself to work through his expression and his performance. The acting teacher and professor Jerry Rojo wrote this about actors: "The essence of acting at the highest level, which arguably has spiritual connotations, is that a performer's entire being exists only to serve the spectator or the art of theatre. Without that quality, the audience easily senses, then rejects the actor, whose professional motives are questionable or self-serving in...an act of prostitution." I feel that the same can be said about both music and musicians.

As the most valuable resource in the world of creative work, expression must be recognized, encouraged, developed, and nurtured—even in those who have no skill in any specific art form. Expression is as universal as it is unique, since it pertains to each person's individual way of informing the rest of the world exactly who they are. Personal expression is the only thing available to people that truly allows them to be free.

This is why it makes no sense to instruct popular musicians to imitate one another or to follow some kind of arbitrary template for repeating the same old ideas over and over as a pathway to success. Forcing all artists to utilize a template that simulates a familiar mode of expression means submerging the substance of everyone's unique, individual expression and invalidates its very meaning.

Over the past twenty to thirty years, an elite group of classic rock records have been turned into templates or archetypes and are regularly being remade in some form or another. On this short list are such chestnuts as *The Joshua Tree* by U2, *Nevermind* by Nirvana, and *Enema of the State* by Blink-182. These recordings were all great in their own right and time. However, they wound up being some of the last original statements created in the genre of rock music, as both artists and business people began treating their work as jobs and taking everything for granted.

Every civilization needs great original statements in popular music, and the only way this civilization will get theirs is if our artists consider the value of true expression and draw from it freely, without inhibition. Without resistance to conformity and fearlessness, all music (and art) will eventually lose its vitality, its relevance and necessity, and recede from public consciousness.

This is where we come back to that line from the Bhagavad Gita, which probably makes a bit more sense now. It is exactly the imperfection of an artist's expression that makes it so flawless, so specific to him. It is also the very thing that guarantees no one may ever hear his name or his work. But because the artist has his own voice, all the more reason for him to use it exactly as it is intended, instead of trying to imitate someone else who may have had tremendous success.

Here are two more lines from the same paragraph, which further underscore this point: "Your resolve is futile if a sense of individuality makes you think 'I shall not fight,' Arjuna—nature will compel you to. You are bound by your own action intrinsic to your being, even against your will you must now do what delusion makes you refuse."

Wow. "Nature will compel you. You are bound by your own action—intrinsic to your being." When I read that, all that comes to mind is this: you have a singular destiny, a path specific to you that you must fulfill.

It is amazing how a few lines from this ancient tract can parallel an eternal truth of creative expression so flawlessly, while telling the story of a mighty warrior. The warrior, named Arjuna, faces an enormous battle against members of his own family, is wracked with conflict, and considers choosing a course of action that is completely contrary to his being. The god Krishna, of whom Ajuna is a great devotee, speaks to him as his advisor, friend, and conscience. He tells Arjuna that to act out of willfulness, out of an emotional reaction and not his intrinsic sense of purpose, goes against his basic nature—that is, not just who he is, but what he is. He is a warrior and cannot avoid that, under any conditions.

For an artist, it is no different. An artist's purpose is to express his unique creative vision through his chosen medium, uniquely. This expression may be imperfect, it may be difficult for others to comprehend, but it is more important that this vision is expressed with integrity than for an artist to ignore his own voice and appropriate someone else's. That is precisely why forcing him to be anything other than what he is, trying to reroute, to subvert, or pervert his creative vision is not only unrealistic but it is also an act against his very nature—and against nature, itself.

14

CREATIVE EXPRESSION AS COMMUNICATION

A while back, I saw the Indian percussionist Zakir Hussain perform with an ensemble of other musicians at the Walt Disney Concert Hall in Los Angeles. It was the first time I'd seen Zakir Hussain, and the first time I'd been to this venue, which boasts some of the finest acoustics in the entire world.

The Disney Concert Hall lived up to its reputation. The acoustics were so accurate that you could hear people murmuring from the opposite balcony, which was several hundred feet away.

Zakir Hussain also lived up to his reputation—the concert was a revelation. The musicians were brilliant and their technique was almost superhuman. At times, it felt like I was being inundated with such a barrage of information that I thought my head was going to spin off my body.

It was apparent that this was something more than a group of people simply playing their instruments. Apart from the raw power that the musicians emanated, I began to notice a constant throbbing pulse that snaked its way through every note they played. No matter how intense the rhythmic subdivisions or their complexity, the players always knew where they were. This pulse was like an invisible force that anchored them together.

At specific points in the performance, the leader would play a complex rhythm, and the other musicians would echo that rhythm back to him on their instruments, exactly as the leader had played it. After this happened a few times, I realized what was really happening. The players, the instruments, the music—it was all a façade. This performance was not an exhibition; it was a refined form of communication at the highest possible level between individuals who had total mastery of their medium.

This is the essence of expression as a medium of communication. Expression pertains not only to a mere outpouring of emotion (which on its own is meaningless and formless) but also to the desire and the ability to communicate it. Expression through art both surpasses and transcends verbal communication. It can evoke specific emotions or sensations in people and, relative to song-based music, it *recontextualizes* lyrics and informs of their true necessity. From this perspective, lyrics become a delivery system for enhancing the mood of a song.

The refinement of expression comes from developing mastery over one's medium. But technical ability is secondary to the ability to emote or impart a mood, which is an innate gift. The greatest artists will learn all the rules about their medium in order to toss out the rule book and create an entirely new expressive language—one that is unique to them alone. This need to learn the rules in order to break them is an element that defined the careers of artists such as Pablo Picasso.

Expression is universal. Every person has the innate ability and the palpable need to express himself in some way. It is a gift that every person possesses no matter who they are—a gift that all are compelled to share and release, whether by communicating verbally with one another, playing an instrument, writing a legal brief, or operating on someone to save his life. As certain people have an ability to express themselves through specialized kinds of work, others have the ability to express themselves through a specific artistic medium.

Unlike many other modes of expression, music and the arts have the power to connect people with a far greater reality than the one that they experience themselves in their day-to-day lives. In a secular society, music and the arts are the nearest connection people have to divinity.

15

COMMUNICATION IN THE CREATIVE ENVIRONMENT

What I find most fun is working with a group of people in a creative setting—especially when everyone is committed to working together to pursue a common vision. Nothing can top that.

I've spent months sequestered in recording studios listening to the same music over and over for days on end. The three things that transform this experience from being utterly tedious into something fun and joyful are a love for the process, a love of the project, and the connection between all the participants. There is an understanding that everyone involved has come together to make something meaningful—something that embodies the essence of all the participants and their unified vision.

The interpersonal and social aspects of recording are fascinating. The way creative people put aside their own personal issues for the common purpose of communicating with one another so that, as a group, they can create something that will communicate to many other people is a unique process unlike any other. This often requires subtle modifications in how all the participants communicate with one another.

Recently, my mom sent me yet another in a long series of forwarded e-mails. Unlike the ones she sent in the past, which featured photos of adorable puppies and kittens, this one was comprised of photos of people, with a quote from Albert Einstein.

The e-mail heading was "Just in case you had any hope for humanity…" The Einstein quote read as follows: "I fear the day when the technology overlaps with our humanity. The world will only have a generation of idiots." The people in the pictures were engaged in various activities, but they all had one thing in common—they were ignoring each other, and enraptured with their mobile phones.

Everyone knows what that looks like. In fact, we've all been there at one time or another. People are constantly speaking and interacting with one another; however, they very seldom *truly* communicate. These days, people actually seem to avoid truly connecting with others, even though there are more avenues of communication than ever before. Instead of an exchange of thoughts or feelings, people tend to talk at one another, through their devices.

Real communication involves sharing feelings, thoughts, ideas, hopes, and fears, and is reflected through whatever expressive medium a person or artist employs. It covers and conveys the full range of human emotion, it is more powerful and encompasses far more than mere verbal language. It also requires a degree of intimacy, which is easily bypassed when people are "speaking" with one another via text or e-mail. People can avoid divulging (or having others detect) changes in vocal stress and facial expression, or even being present, spontaneous, and honest in a conversation.

Oddly enough, there are few places in this world where the lack of intimacy and honesty is more obvious than in a recording studio. A lot of talking goes on there, but too often there is no real interaction between individuals, and virtually no honesty.

This is because:

1. People are often afraid of inadvertently offending other people by giving an honest assessment of what they are doing. Sometimes it is easier to tell others what they want to hear instead of what they need to hear. I feel that this is partly because of rampant codependency and a pervasive fear of potentially being replaced. No one wants to lose his job and be humiliated in the process.

2. People are often afraid of being wrong—especially in front of others. This usually happens when someone says the wrong thing to the wrong person at the wrong time. Consequently, people are generally disinclined to speak up even when they feel compelled to do so. No one wants to look bad, be out of line, or be reprimanded.

3. People often don't have the technical ability or the skill to assess another person and give helpful feedback. In this case, a person may feel better saying nothing at all than to betray the fact that he doesn't know what he's doing. No one wants to look like an idiot in front of people they're supposed to be directing.

4. People often think that by focusing only on positive aspects of someone's work, they are providing assistance via positive reinforcement. Although positive reinforcement is helpful at the right time, if that is all they receive, they are not getting the whole truth.

5. Being honest also entails a commitment. If you critique someone else's work, you are also creating a blank, open space, which you are then responsible for filling in. By commenting on a specific problem, you make yourself responsible for providing a solution. This requires doing work and making an effort.

Honesty can be a double-edged sword—the truth can be painful. However, in the long run, honesty is a gift we offer and share with others. By being honest, we are also sharing our feelings. This is the essence of communication.

Honesty is also a gift to ourselves. The more honest we are about how we feel, the more we are demonstrating our own self-respect. In this world, feeling is a luxury that people seldom afford themselves—as is true self-respect.

Total honesty and open communication requires total fearlessness without the guarantee of reciprocation. This means opening yourself up to another person—and if the connection made is real, the person with whom you are communicating must open himself up to you. Being truthful requires vulnerability on both sides. It is the ultimate surrender.

Communication between producer and artist helps establish an artist's ability to perform and communicate with an audience. This part of their relationship is a kind of role-play exercise. It must be clear to the artist that if through his performance he can make the producer believe in what he is doing, he will be able to convince anyone. Although the producer is a scrupulous judge of the artist's performance, he is nowhere near as harsh a critic as the public.

As a group, the public has a short attention span. You can lose them forever in less than ten seconds—and they vote with their pocketbooks. If you can get their attention, feel blessed. Once you have their attention, the onus is on you to keep it.

When creative people come together in a creative space, they bring their personal lives and remnants of their entire life experience with them. With them, also come their subliminal issues, their psychology, and the multitude of personalities that they embody. Their personalities and issues subsequently interact with the personalities and issues of everyone else in the creative work space.

It seems to me that everyone has multiple personalities. There's the personality we want to project, and the personality we truly have. For example, I always wanted to be seen as a tough guy, but I'm really more of a nerd.

Then, there's the personality that corresponds to how we believe our parents see us and the one that corresponds to how we believe others see us. Along with all those personalities, it can be said that each of us carries a child within. This child exists in suspended animation—frozen at a moment in time when he was traumatized in some way and, consequently, never grew up. This child is innocent, charming, conniving, and malicious, and has his own agenda, which is often invisible to the adult it inhabits. Often, we have several children within us, all locked into a moment when they were wounded in some way and have never been able to grow from that point. One part of the creative process is acknowledging the inner child and freeing it from this catatonic, suspended state.

As if by sending invisible tentacles into the creative space, the child within us interacts with the children in other people around us. It tests the environment to see who is nearby, how they like to play, and how they will interact with us.

When personalities interact, I feel there is also a subtle dynamic that takes place beneath the surface of normal engagement: each individual assumes a subliminal personality or archetype above and beyond his basic personality. These subliminal personalities are often a revisitation of the child in each person. If you're really sensitive to this dynamic, you can sometimes see a picture in your mind's eye of what each person looked like as a child.

On one project, I recorded with a musician in his home studio. He lived there with his wife, a roommate, and a revolving cast of nameless spectral characters who'd constantly file in and out of this surreal studio-cum-domestic environment like human tumbleweeds.

This was quite a place. It was a house and a recording studio all in one, each fighting moment by moment for ultimate hegemony. There was gear everywhere. One room was a repository for old broken instruments, stacked up sideways against one wall and piled high against another. In every corner of the house, chaos reigned supreme. I noticed that among the many things this person collected were books from when he was a small child. There were kitschy paintings of fantasy scenes that combined historical eras and fairy tales in a disquieting mélange of blues, yellows, and pinks. It felt like this was an elaborate façade, unconsciously concocted to re-create a warped sense of the family this guy had lost or never had.

One day the whole thing became glaringly obvious. Another man's home might be his castle, but this man's home/studio was his clubhouse. He was Peter Pan, his wife was Wendy, and his extended family of friends and roommates were the Lost Boys. He and his wife even looked like two children when they were together.

Holy mackerel—I was recording in Neverland!

When people interact, some are alpha, or dominant, and some are submissive. Some are peacemakers and some are antagonists. Some change into character completely when they enter a creative space and transform back the minute they leave that space. Some people completely modify who they are, depending on who they're around, from moment to moment.

In many cases, people unconsciously assume these personalities in order to re-create an ancient, familiar dynamic or to heal an old wound that has never been resolved. They also exist or are invoked to interact in a familiar way with the archetypes of other people whose behavior is a "call" that demands a specific response.

When you're working with other people in a creative space, it is often necessary to intuit each person's needs and their personal dynamic. It is also helpful to observe their interactions with one another to determine if there is animosity or acrimony. Once the interpersonal relationships are out in the open, the producer will understand how to help the participants work most efficiently through any issues that might emerge while they are working together.

It can be very easy for the producer to get inadvertently pulled into the undertow of this subliminal and emotional interaction (as it is for everyone else in the creative space), because they address primitive, emotional characteristics of behavior. However, it is essential that instead of reacting to this stimulus, the producer stays neutral and an observer at all times.

By relying on his practices of meditation and patience, the producer can slow his perception of the events unfolding around him down to a crawl and remain neutral, experiencing and objectifying emotions without reacting to them. This is another mindfulness exercise that is similar to the way he might deal with an artist who is upset. By going within and listening only to what his inner voice is telling him, the producer will better understand what is happening around him. Instead of reacting, the producer does nothing. By doing nothing, he creates a null or neutral space around himself.

Building neutral space gradually affects the creative environment and can encourage a positive connection between everyone involved. Neutralizing the immediate environment is a way of breaking a chain of dysfunctional interaction, which has been an all-too-familiar component in band dynamics.

Learning to read an artist's behavioral "tells" by watching facial expressions and body language or listening for vocal or verbal cues can also be helpful in the production and facilitation process. Through a combination of verbal, physical, and behavioral mannerisms, a person can tell everything about himself, whether he has consciously chosen to or not.

On a fundamental level, most people hide behind some sort of façade, but actually want to be perceived for who they truly are. This is because they want to identify themselves and to locate others like them so that they can reestablish their tribe.

The other reason is that most people don't really want to conceal anything, even if they're hiding terrible or embarrassing secrets about themselves. Often, there is an instinctive need to release hidden information, as it requires immense effort to conceal and hold on to it. It also takes up unnecessary space within an individual's psyche—space that is better used to deal with things in the present.

This is one reason why, under the right conditions, most people will divulge their secrets. Therefore, it is imperative to maintain a relaxed, open creative environment just in case the artist needs the space to have a breakthrough and communicate who he truly is.

THE DYNAMICS OF WHO'S ON THE TOP AND WHO'S ON THE BOTTOM

Doing creative work with a group of people is awesome, although sometimes, it can also bring up personal issues for certain individuals.

You'd think that in an ideal world, you'd experience a complete sense of equality with everyone you interact with, creatively and otherwise. While that dynamic does happen occasionally, it is generally the exception and not the rule. More often you will encounter individuals who prefer their relationships (creative and otherwise) to be out of balance.

People like these define their relationships by immediately establishing who holds the power and who doesn't. This is probably a survival skill that traces all the way back to when our feral ancestors had to intuit which was the alpha animal in their group. Animals need to know who the leader is. They need to know who's eating first, who's mating first, and who should not be challenged unless it's time for a new leader.

Human beings have their own unique ways of establishing primacy over one another. It appears that people need either to be dominated or to dominate one another; they generally do not regard one another as being equal. While there is often a need for leaders in creative situations, there is no real need for a specific individual to express needless dominance over the others. This type of dynamic is counterproductive and irrelevant to the creative process.

As rational animals that think and feel, we have evolved past basic survival needs and are capable of interacting in groups without primitive role-play games or shows of force.

Or are we?

WHEN THE GUITARIST MET THE PRODUCER (A CAUTIONARY TALE)

Once upon a time, I produced a recording for a band. This band came from a magical land far, far away where everyone spoke with funny accents and lived in opulent houses in sequestered, gated communities. In keeping with the unusual customs of this land, the ruler of this band was not the vocalist (as is normally the case), but the guitarist. This guitarist wrote about 90 percent of the band's songs, created all the parts for the rest of the musicians in the band, made all the decisions, threw his weight around mercilessly, and ruled over his dominion with an iron fist.

The guitarist treated everyone else in his band—including the singer—as though they were nothing more than extensions of himself. For the recording I was going to produce, the guitarist had meticulously prepared song demos with even more meticulously mapped-out vocal performances, and he insisted the vocalist replicate them precisely, down to the tone, phrasing—even the ad-libs.

To me, the guitarist appeared to be a complete perfectionist and a consummate pro. I was impressed by the sense of order he'd created in his domain and thought it would be refreshing to work with someone who was so attentive to minute details.

Within a few months of recording, my blinders came off. In a word, I'd been *had*.

One prerequisite to producing this recording was that I had to share a coproduction credit with the guitarist. Having done so on prior records, I knew this was mainly a vanity credit and that the other artists who had the same stipulation on previous recordings had very little understanding of record production.

Without hesitation, I agreed, was hastily contracted, and then we got to work.

Once we began production, it became apparent that this coproduction credit was not what I'd believed it to be. When combined with the guitarist's position as supreme ruler of his band, the coproduction credit gave him carte blanche over every aspect of the project. He had consolidated his power and now held dominion over us all. And from that point forth, as far as he was concerned, he—and not me—was actually producing the record.

But then, why did he want a producer at all? Over time, the answer to this question became clear. He didn't want one for any of the practical reasons one would expect. He didn't really care if a producer enhanced the quality of his record—he knew that would happen anyway. He certainly didn't care about having an objective outsider who could help him step his game up a few notches or give him a new perspective and clarity regarding his work.

The guitarist really wanted a producer so he could have another person to dominate, in the same way he dominated his band and everyone else who came into his orbit. This made him feel comfortable and it seemed to be the only kind of relationship he understood.

In his life, someone always had to be on top and someone else always had to be on the bottom. And since the person on top always had to be him, who better to dominate than the very person he'd hired to direct his recording?

Among the material we were recording, there was one song in particular that everyone really liked, including myself. It was the one piece of music that seemed to be genuine and elicited a positive response from everyone who heard it. In hindsight, I feel as though some powerful sadistic tendencies that lay submerged beneath the guitarist's veneer of control and order were probably agitated awake when I let him know how passionately I felt about his song. Whatever happened, his subsequent behavior was something I'd never seen before.

Shortly thereafter, the guitarist randomly began to ponder shelving this song for a "Greatest Hits" album, instead of recording it for this one. Instantly, everyone on the project began to panic and begged him to reconsider. Order was eventually restored, but it wasn't long before the seeds of discord were sown yet again. This was no longer about saving the song for a future record—out of the blue, the guitarist stated with absolute conviction that the song wasn't working for him and he began to tinker with random sections of it.

Of course, this song had been pored over relentlessly in preproduction and the consensus had been that it worked and was ready to be recorded. As expected, this new piece of news was a shock and caused everyone to return to their previous state of panic. This project had become transformed from a joint creative undertaking into a nightmarish battle of wills and everyone involved was now in a constant state of protracted anxiety. The guitarist was making it agonizingly clear that he would go as far as vivisecting his own creations to demonstrate that he, and only he, was in control of the ship. He was not only the king of this band, but also the Keiser Soze (check out the scene in *The Usual Suspects*, where someone describes how this character sacrificed his entire family over his honor) of rock.

The guitarist's issue with the song focused on its second bridge, which had a vocal melody that was a variation on an earlier bridge melody. This bridge also came to a dead stop at its final bar, after which, the song built back up to a chorus tag out.

This bridge added nice dynamics and a little drama. It also worked well with the narrative of the song. Somehow, this bridge became a no-man's land for which the utterly senseless battle over this now brutalized song was fought.

After allowing the bridge section's fate to teeter in the balance for a month (and with it, the nerves of every other participant on the recording), the guitarist finally made his move. He presented an entirely new bridge to replace the original.

On hearing it, my first question was—what? And my second question was—why? Apart from going to half-time, the new part had no dynamics, no chord modulation, no melody—vocal or otherwise—it was lifeless and mechanical. It also struck me as a head-scratchingly bad choice considering what it was replacing.

To a man, everyone else on the project was mortified by this completely irrational and senseless alteration. The new bridge not only ruined the functionality of the song, but also the primary point of release would now occur too late. Trying to incorporate this new bridge also meant that instruments would need to be rerecorded in order for it to exist in the song.

Like before, the milled throng of serfs gathered to kiss the guitarist's ring, begging him to reconsider his harsh choice, but this time his mind was made up. It was going to be his way or no way.

In the end, the guitarist got his second bridge just the way he wanted it. He dominated his band, defeated his producer, won the war, and proved that he was forever and always in control. Once again, he was on top.

In the end, it appears that was all that really mattered to him.

16

DELUSIONAL THINKING FROM THE DEPTHS OF THE MUSIC BUSINESS AND BEYOND

The following statements have been either overheard in passing, expressed in essence, or discussed outright. Many people apparently believe that

- Music is a passive experience and a background accompaniment instead of a foreground experience that actively engages the listener.
- Music is an incidental (as opposed to being an irreplaceable) part of their lives.
- Although music might at one time have served a vital function in society as a form of artistic expression, it no longer has the same value or meaning (and might not ever again). Sometimes, when addressing other people who feel more passionately about music than they do, they make comments trivializing it like, "Hey, it's just music."
- Music should be free. This doesn't just mean that music should be acquired without compensating the artist who made it (because it's essentially valueless to anyone); it also signifies that the artist is seen as not having put enough effort into his or her work to make it worthwhile (which has essentially made it valueless to everyone who hears it).

- What's good is actually "great," and what's mediocre is actually "good." This explains why there is such a preponderance of mediocre popular music and nothing truly great.
- A bad-sounding recording with sampled drums, thin-sounding, compressed guitars, and Auto-Tuned vocals is better than a well-recorded, warm-sounding recording with unadulterated instrumental and vocal performances. Interestingly, because bad recordings have become the rule rather than the exception, many listeners (as well as people who work in record companies) feel this way.
- Singers whose vocals are Auto-Tuned actually sound like that and sing that way. This is why a lot of newer singers have begun unconsciously emulating the effects of an Auto-Tuned vocal when they perform—for example, unnaturally sliding from note to note—as a natural vocal phrasing technique.

Many people who work in record and tech companies believe that

- People are followers by nature. They see the general public as an enormous flock of sheep, which have no intrinsic value apart from being consumers.
- There are formulas that can be used to create music. In this model, music exists solely as a product (like a widget built on an assembly line), has a basic assignable value, and is universally embraced and purchased by everyone.
- These industries can rely on audiences possessing increasingly diminishing attention spans. This is one reason record companies continue to release recordings of diminishing

value and quality. They seem to be unaware that the Frankenstein they built is out of control, and that by catering to the lowest common societal denominator, these companies have created the very problem that is presently annihilating their business.

- Artists are a resource that exists to be dominated, controlled, and exploited.
- The job of making music involves producers and artists working agonizingly hard, following to the letter rules that they didn't create, and that have nothing to do with them or the creation of music.

Many people believe that there are tangible, market-based explanations for how and why the music business is falling apart. None of these explanations has anything to do with the quality (or lack thereof) of the product the record companies are offering.

Many people outside the music industry believe that the quality of music being produced nowadays is beneath their contempt. These people come from many different age groups and are capable of thinking for themselves.

There is clearly a disconnect between these people and the music business people who perceive them as the demographics they must conquer. Why is this so?

17

HARMONIC LAYERING AND THE CREATIVE USE OF DISTORTION

I love sound. I love noise. I love hearing the sounds of instruments coming out of loudspeakers after being transduced through microphones or heavily modified through weird electronic processing. I love tonality, texture, and dynamics as a means to enhance an emotional state or mood more perfectly. As far as I'm concerned, these elements can't ever be made too extreme or too unusual.

Creating instrumental sounds that exist in a specific tonal range, have unusual tonal characteristics, and interact in a way that creates a unique fusion is one of the most satisfying and emotional experiences one can have making music. By constructing sonic landscapes in this way, I get to experience the tripled pleasure of having created something tonally unique, something that evokes a powerful mood while embodying and enhancing the artist's intent, and something that just sounds cool.

Sound has a visceral quality and is the vehicle by which people encounter music. With this in mind, I am completely baffled by anyone who asserts that good sound is an unnecessary component in recorded popular music.

Compressed audio is popular because it makes large quantities of music available to anyone whenever and however they want it. Unfortunately, due to the nature of compressed audio files, large chunks of resolution are lost, along with a great deal of the integrity and intent that were present in the making of a piece of music. Without the entire sonic picture, we, the listeners, are deprived of some of the magic that was formerly there.

I was recently told that every few months a very well-known speaker manufacturer rents out Abbey Road's enormous Studio One for a special program exclusively for schoolchildren. The day is spent with these kids experiencing every aspect of listening, and through a variety of different speaker systems. These outings climax with music that, after being heard on a variety of smaller speakers, is played through the manufacturer's flagship speakers—which conveniently happen to be the studio's mains. Because of the detail of these speakers and their superior ability to reproduce music, this experience winds up being absolutely life changing for these children.

Sound is all around us. Our ears and nervous systems are responding to sounds from moment to moment. Music is organized sound, and sound is inseparable from music, so it follows that making a recording sound extraordinary should be vitally important. It also stands to reason that people respond to varying degrees of sound quality. When musicians record their performances onto substandard, poor-sounding tracks, their performances are also substandard. When they have the opportunity to work on and be captured by great-sounding recordings, they are inspired and their performances are enhanced tremendously.

We are generally influenced in great part by what we grew up listening to. In other words, we listen to what we are creating, and create what we are listening to based on what we have become familiar with, and what was influential to us formatively.

The pop music I grew up listening to was primarily the Beatles. Those records were the technological marvels of their day. They were created meticulously. As Beatles records became more experimental, the band also began to push the existing recording technology further. The group's constant creative explorations drove them to create sonic combinations that had never before been attempted, and which provoked the maximum emotional response from the listener.

The Beatles were influenced not only by the culture and current events at that time (all of which found their way into the group's music) but also by a wide variety of other music, by composers such as Karlheinz Stockhausen and John Cage, who had spent years pushing the outer limits of sonic creation.

As is always the case, these influences leached into the Beatles' food chain, trickling down to me and everyone else who listened to their records. In this way, I was indirectly influenced by the approaches to instrumental layering, texture, and usage of distortion that these composers had developed. I also liked watching war movies, such as *The Longest Day*, because I found the sounds of things exploding very…stimulating. With that groundwork laid, when I was directly exposed to Stockhausen, Cage, et al, much later on, I was more open to them. As a result of my influences, I tend to gravitate toward combinations of instruments that are not only unusual, but also meaningful and emotionally compelling.

I have never been interested in merely faithfully reproducing an artist's sound as accurately as possible. That approach is akin to a classic painter who enjoys painting the same tedious landscape over and over, and I find it impossible to relate to. I thrive on examining each component part of a musical statement, understanding its importance and context within the structure of a piece of music, shaping a voice for said component that amplifies these characteristics, and sonically placing it so it has relevance, meaning and a proper role in relation to the whole musical picture. I feel each sound must occupy its own unique space while working together with other sounds to create an even more compelling sonic matrix.

Instead of looking at what's in front of me and accepting it at face value, I want to feel it as deeply as possible. In doing this, I'm consciously aware of trying to design a sonic structure whereby anyone listening to the finished product will immediately feel the same thing I do.

I am always compelled to go deep inside whatever I'm working on and find its true meaning—to go far beneath the surface and discover every ounce of ugliness and beauty within. It's never enough simply to imitate what you hear; the greater challenge is to find the emotional source and then represent that emotion instead of its manifestation.

This is something that makes record production fascinating— the process of finding and describing an emotion through combinations of sounds instead of recording a bunch of instruments and trying to make them sound passable together.

There is always an emotional code to be cracked when recording an artist's work. One part of that code can often be revealed through the sonic choices made in the recording. In a recording, sound—given proper care and consideration— reflects and amplifies emotion.

I find that people tend to build recordings according to their impression of the style of music they are working in. Hence, when making a record that is mainly acoustic guitar and vocal, the emphasis is primarily on soft-sounding acoustic guitars and breathy, soft vocals. The sounds are recorded similarly, with soft-sounding microphones and smooth-sounding signal processing.

This approach has never worked for me, because I feel it removes any potential for subtext and other emotional elements that can create exciting, engaging tension.

In my world, contrast is both essential and stunning. For example, it can be fun, disconcerting, and utterly called for to drop a disturbingly ugly element into the context of a gorgeous piece of music. After all, we are trying to communicate emotional content to other people, and isn't life abundant with extremes and opposites?

In order to create extremes, I like experimenting with such diversity as variable transient responses in instruments, beautiful textural elements, intense dynamics, and sounds that have great detail yet are extremely distorted by a variety of different means. By combining these (and other) elements in different ways, the producer ensures that the recording process is never boring and the same record can never be made twice. Working this way relies on spontaneity—taking sensory impressions of music and converting them into soundscapes. It also requires acumen, time, and commitment.

To me, the incorporation of distortion is a crucial aspect of recording any kind of popular music. Much that is sonically pleasing about recordings made using analog recording equipment results from the fact that these devices are not only flawed, but they also have unique characteristics and color the sound with audible amounts of harmonic distortion.

I want to be clear about what I mean when I use the word "distortion." To some people, "distortion" signifies ugliness or warping the appearance of something; I see it as a means for shading and adding specific character to an instrument tone. In my world, distortion can cover a vast range, from virtually undetectable to a wall of noise, and, like a flavoring, is used accordingly to taste.

There are unlimited types of distortion, from vacuum tubes to transistors to solid state—even digital distortion. Each sounds different, and all are worth investigating. I like to drive virtually every instrument I record to the point of perceptual, audible distortion. I will do this at every stage of amplification, not just because it sounds better to me, but because I feel the aesthetic intent demonstrates a kind of desperation, an urgency to communicate directly and immediately with a listener. As stated earlier, this approach is meant to be expressive and convey emotion, not simply to reproduce a sound.

Layering sounds and textures is an art form that relies on the range in which an instrument is played, among other things. When using a group of highly distorted instrument sounds together, I find it is important to pay close attention to where and how they sit relative to one another. For example, when placing a heavily distorted keyboard sound in relation to a heavily distorted electric guitar, it's very easy to lose one or both and create mud if range, register, and tone aren't considered. Orchestration and chord choices become very important in a completely different way, since there is a wider array of harmonics that speak completely differently from the way they would if there were no distortion.

The name of the game is coexistence. If the instrument sounds can't work together interdependently or in a larger sonic matrix, they don't belong in the recording.

When considering range, it's important to take into account the overall tonal picture and the foundation you are building onto. If the drums are big, fat, and punchy; the cymbals are bright and aggressive; and the bass is deep, full, throaty, and a bit fuzzy—you already have a large sonic stage. How can anything else fit, and where can you put it?

A big bass sound will often extend into the tonal range of the guitars. This means that the guitar will need to occupy its own space away from the bass. Otherwise, the two will fight for prominence. This issue may be further compounded if the guitar is playing in a low register.

There are many ways to deal with this issue. First is considering what the function of the guitar is, rhythmically and texturally. Next is how best to get this across with the technology at your disposal and make the desired emotional statement.

It is helpful to learn to visualize the sound. I use this approach to "see" how the instrument tones sit together, developing a visual reference for each of them, and visualizing how new tones will interact with the current tones.

One of the most prominent parts of a bass sound is its roundness and depth. It moves air. Many of its notes exist in the same general vicinity as a bass drum. In fact, on many English recordings from the 1960s and '70s, the bass guitar was often intended to occupy a lower tonal position than the bass drum. As full and round as a guitar sound may be, it will never have the same depth or move the same amount of air as a bass guitar. It is then a simple matter of establishing the bass and guitar as two separate entities, yet entities that must coexist and interact gracefully. From a musical standpoint, a guitar may play in the same pitch range as the bass, but it may not work being perceived sonically in the same tonal range.

I often try to envision the recording as a three-dimensional field with different textures that also have different depths, densities, and shapes. Sometimes a narrow, gritty texture will work best when flanked by two enormous, dense, deep textures.

Listening to what you've already recorded and finding the spaces that need filling will always provide the best guidelines and direct you to where you need to go. You'll do your best work when you are mindful of what's happening in the present.

As the orchestration of a song develops, the greater textural and tonal picture begins to emerge. Although it may appear that there are many sonic choices regarding instrument sounds, the truth is that if your goal is to create a specific emotional statement for a piece of music, the choices are very few. I find the creative work is in how best to realize them.

18

THE CONTRACT

The contract is an important tool with which to establish the artist's focus and maintain his awareness of the commitment he is making to his own work. This is not a legal document or a specific work agreement, but more of a mission statement.

The contract can serve as a reference point for the artist whenever he strays from his objective. It is effective because it is usually a written document that the artist himself has signed.

The contract itself should be a few sentences or paragraphs that affirm the intent and goals of the artist going forward into a new endeavor. The contract should be written using language that is comprehensible, personal, and specific to the artist and his needs. In this way, the contract becomes even more significant and meaningful to the artist.

The contract can include humor—even colorful language (if this is relative and pertinent to the artist)—and it must adhere to his specific guidelines. At the bottom, it will be signed and dated by the artist. This will further affirm the finality and resolve of the artist's commitment. This sort of contract also adds immeasurably to the dramatic/ritualistic value of the experience. It has weight.

People tend to respond differently when something is presented to them in a concrete form, instead of as an abstract proposition. Seeing the terms of his work written out as a mission statement or a declaration, the artist will view the contract as a profound affirmation.

The contract can be displayed in a prominent place in the artist's creative space as a constant reminder. In this way, the contract becomes a symbol of the creative process as an abstract idea, now made concrete and "engraved in stone."

19

THE INNER VOICE
AND THE FIRST STEP

Here's a question: If your job description consists primarily of letting your imagination run wild, why would you possibly let this experience metamorphose into feeling as though you're on an assembly line? That sounds tedious, doesn't it? Now, I may be missing something, but isn't imagination allergic to tedium?

When people first start a recording project, they generally gravitate toward one of two roles, which become an identity or a mask that can supersede the basic personality of its owner. One role is submissive, whereby the individual is looking for guidance and is expecting to be directed. This is often the mind-set of the artist. The other role is a dominant one, whereby the individual is prepared to control and dictate to everyone else. This is often the producer/technician's mind-set. Occasionally, the roles are reversed and the artist attempts to dominate the creative space, and sometimes the producer/technician is looking to be directed.

Now, let's imagine a hypothetical situation in which we forget about roles, dominance, submission, and assembly lines. Let's pretend instead that everyone coming into the recording session is on the same page with each other.

Let's imagine that there is an awareness between all the participants that entering the recording studio environment is simply a logical extension of the creative collaboration that the participants have so far been willingly and openly engaged in.

Let's also imagine that everyone on the recording project is operating from the same intent, with the same goals, and there are no egos or hidden personal agendas involved.

What a wonderful and perfect working environment this is. It is fertile and will yield further great collaborations and great results.

Now, let's consider the actual music this team of fraternally spirited individuals is working on. It evokes feeling and emotion. That is to say, it makes whoever hears it feel something specific. There is a palpable mood—an emotion to it that may vary from listener to listener, but will always be present.

Because of its immeasurable value and necessity, this sensation and the need to represent it accurately has been noted and consciously developed from early on in the creative collaborative process by everyone involved. Without this feeling, music is just a clutter of annoying sounds, clumsily thrown together by careless dilettantes who don't care about what they are doing, and have made no meaningful investment in it.

People experience music in many ways. Not only can it be experienced in figurative terms (like memories, moods, and emotions), but it can also be experienced in visceral terms (as physical sensations that occur in one's body).

One way to verify this is to sit and listen to a particularly compelling piece of music—one that you find moving and exciting, or one that consistently elicits a specific emotion in you when you listen to it. To do this properly, there can be no distractions, nothing that can deter you from the simple act of being present.

As you listen to the music, in addition to your understanding of the mood or emotion you are experiencing, you will begin to notice that you are also experiencing physical sensations. What do these sensations feel like? How do you experience them? They could manifest as a tightening in your throat, a warm sensation in your chest, an unidentifiable (yet strangely pleasurable) feeling that starts behind your jaw and moves down through the top portion of your body.

I can't say exactly how this manifests in anyone else—I only know for sure what happens to me. Each person experiences this in a completely different way. There is no right, no wrong, just feeling.

Once you're aware of these physical sensations, it's helpful to take some time and to reflect on them. You can recall these feelings, these emotions and physical sensations, not specifically by describing them with words—although it might be interesting to write about the experience in a journal—but simply by recalling how the experience felt, where in your body you felt it, what emotions this feeling may have elicited from you, and, if you wanted, what could cause this feeling to arise in the future.

These sensations have a purpose. They exist as a touchstone, a reference point, a bookmark that we can return to when we're doing creative work. These sensations also act as a bridge: a means of communing with one's subconscious. They illuminate a place inside each person that reveals their unadulterated truth.

Now, imagine that you're on a lovely, relaxing vacation lying in a hammock beside a translucent green ocean that sports languid, rolling waves while gentle zephyrs play across your motionless body.

You're lounging about in this idyllic paradise and your mind is drifting off into oblivion when suddenly, from the distant recesses of your subconscious, almost imperceptibly, you hear the vague stirrings of a far-off melody, whispering to you. But this isn't just any melody. It sounds vaguely familiar but, within a single heartbeat, you realize that it's actually something you've never heard before.

And it's absolutely wonderful.

You know what happens next. Your head begins to spin. You struggle to your feet and search for the nearest instrument you can find. Fortuitously enough, even though you're in the midst of this tropical paradise, there just happens to be a guitar or keyboard (or computer with a conveniently accessible music composition program) on hand for moments such as these.

And right then, with the tool of your choice, you are transformed into a creative midwife—birthing the siren song that gestated in your subconscious before it enters into this temporal world.

While this is taking place, without even being aware, you have become infused with those previously referenced physical sensations—perhaps a multitude of them. While you are busy transcribing the music that is coming to you from deep within, simultaneously you are also experiencing chills, tingling, and all manner of other sensations in your body. Some of these sensations occur instantaneously and dissipate. Some linger. Some are barely perceptible, and some are overwhelming.

This is a powerful sensory experience. Nothing else in the world exists but you, your awareness, and the music, which is now desperately forcing itself out of you.

Nothing else matters.

In the world of creative expression, what is right? What is wrong? These are merely subjective and imaginary positions, opposing points that can't truly be explained by one person to another unless they can somehow be mutually experienced simultaneously in a shared reality. However, relative to a medium such as music, the subjective nature of right (and wrong) can be experienced through sensations, instead of being explained through ideas.

As an individual, you have your own personal built-in, intuitive sense of right and wrong. You may understand what *right* and *wrong* mean to you as intellectual constructs, but more important, you instinctively know what *right* feels like to you—as a sensation—and what feels *wrong*. In other words, you can access the sensory awareness of these concepts and experience what right and wrong feel like in a completely unique, personal way.

This inner world of sensation exists for the benefit of us all, so that we may gain a deeper understanding of ourselves. This inner world also exists for artists so that they can be more creative, more flexible, and better explorers. By being aware of the subtleties of these sensations, we are better able to comprehend their highly specific and personal meanings.

Often, because we are attuned to verbal communication, these sensory messages from within are often experienced in our minds via words, or as an "inner voice." What this inner voice says to each individual is unique, and is for that person alone to decipher. This voice may be telling one person to stop; it may tell someone else to go. It may be telling someone that they need to relax today, or it may be answering a question that has been posed to it internally. Whatever the substance is of each message, it is up to the individual to pay attention, to understand and to learn from them.

One thing that you can develop from being attentive to this inner voice is how to trust your own intuition above anything else. When someone (especially someone who, for whatever reason, you're supposed to listen to) makes a statement that you agree with on a rational level but that also creates a nagging sense of doubt, you'll be more able to discern between the two by listening to these sensations within yourself. By using this inner voice, it is often easier to objectively listen to input from others and determine if it actually works for you.

Being attentive to what you're feeling also means being more flexible than you ever imagined you could be. This means enhancing your imagination and your ability to be creative, being open to crazy, new ideas, and being able to stop on a dime and change your direction in a split second, if need be.

Inflexibility, standing on ceremony, and stubbornness are all equivalent to rigidity, and as it was stated previously, rigidity is the killer of creativity.

Here are a few guidelines to work from when using your "inner voice":

1. Learn what your intuition sounds and feels like and trust it implicitly.
2. You don't need to follow conventional wisdom; you can simply incorporate it into your process where you feel it applies.
3. You don't need to let someone else convince you that you must do things "their way," especially when every cell in your body is telling you that they're wrong.
4. There is a big difference between ego and intuition. Has someone ever casually made a constructive suggestion or a comment to you about something you're doing, and you

instantly became irritated with this person? Going a step further, did you react to what this person may have said in an openly aggressive or hostile manner? Did you ever ask yourself why you reacted in this way? How would it feel if you had taken the comment without reacting and, instead, considered it from an objective perspective, while also paying attention to how your body (not your emotions) felt about it?

5. As you listen to what others say, learn to *feel* what they're saying, as well as *hear* what they're saying. How do the words that a specific person is saying make you feel? How do you feel when you're around this person? Learn to experience the person, as well as his words. In this way, you can better understand yourself.

Sometimes, invoking this process requires taking an initial step. This initial step may be difficult—it may require you to move way outside of a very comfortable and easy perception of the world you inhabit. It doesn't matter what that step is—it's simply a means of demonstrating your own commitment to a deeper truth. By doing this, you are demonstrating this commitment to only one person—yourself.

You can take that first step right now, if you truly wish.

Who can say where you'll wind up? No matter what, I can promise you this: if you take the first step to move out of your familiar zone of comfort and into a deeper experience of the world around you, that first step will eventually lead you to a place you never expected to be, but a place you always imagined you'd be—and, if you're lucky, a place you always hoped you'd be.

Right now, shut out everything around you and still your mind. Allow your muscles to begin gradually relaxing and releasing all their tension. Close your eyes and let your attention move within.

20

HOW DO YOU PERCEIVE SOUND?

God, I hated high school. It was the worst time of my life. I was a terrible student. Raging hormones were running my life into the ground and, frankly, I had no idea why I was learning about things like algebra, which would never be useful unless one dark, moonless night in some dark, nameless alley, an anonymous, delinquent math-murderer put a gun to my head and demanded my life as forfeit unless I could tell him the value of x where $x > 0 > pi/2$.

Meanwhile, the bizarre fantasy that had dogged me for as long as I could recall was to first indulge all my perverted pubescent urges, then eat a veritable mountain of sugar and, finally, sequester myself away in an airless room doing nothing but playing with an enormous modular synthesizer—the edges of which vanished into distant vistas of fog—until I dwindled away to nothing.

However, in spite of this, I was forced to face a harsh reality. The only way I would ever achieve my fantasy was if I escaped high school. Given the appalling state of my grades, this possibility appeared more and more remote. I was forced to consider a more unorthodox route out of the system.

While doggedly attempting to free myself from the dismal confines of high school, I wound up enrolling at an alternative learning establishment called City-As-School (or CAS). It was created on an unusual premise: that some kids (many of whom would probably have been prescribed Ritalin thirty years later) couldn't thrive in a traditional school environment and would learn better in a "nontraditional learning environment." Nontraditional, my ass.

CAS used the term *resources* to describe these nontraditional learning environments. One of my so-called resources was the now defunct Soho Weekly News, where I helped a nice lady organize the classifieds. Another was a woodworking business where I got busted on the first day for trying to steal a little wooden jewelry box for my mom. After going to a couple of these resources I decided that they were little more than slave labor programs for the many dropouts and burnouts looking for a quick ticket out of high school.

At this point in life, I was living on the streets and didn't care how I got a diploma, as long as I got more time to do whatever I wanted. Being a no-good, shiftless ragamuffin, I was unconcerned with doing anything substantive in life—at that time, life was either about playing or brooding. In spite of my youthful nonchalance, cynicism, and overall lack of direction, the single most formative event of my high school years occurred at one of these CAS resources.

I elected to take a music appreciation course at the Manhattan School of Music, one of the few resources you had to go to a classroom for. The teacher was a crusty old gentleman who looked as though he'd been teaching there since the building's cornerstone had been laid. He didn't seem to appreciate the snot-nosed punks who populated his class any more than they liked him.

The other kids in this class clearly felt that being in CAS had somehow insulated them from normalcy. The way they saw it, they'd very bravely dropped out of the traditional school system and thereby, traded up from being in stuffy classrooms with antique teachers and antique fluorescent lighting.

Most of these kids had picked this class because it was called "music appreciation." They appreciated music just fine, so long as it was loud, less than fifteen years old, and wasn't written by some dead guy who hailed from Vienna, Sienna, or Paris.

Once my youthful peers realized they were there to appreciate all kinds of music (and not just Yes or Black Sabbath), most of them must have felt as if they'd been had. A palpable air of bitterness gradually pervaded the class and several motley miscreants began regularly mouthing off at the teacher.

Of course, most of them would just daydream, staring off into space and counting the moments until they could once again find themselves at the Central Park Bandshell smoking pot, commiserating with their lowlife, protohuman cronies, while attempting to acquire exotic venereal diseases and, simultaneously, play Frisbee.

We languished in this class together, juvenile delinquents one and all. We suffered through centuries of music history and were occasionally treated to the odd snatch of song. Much as I didn't want to admit it, I was actually learning something.

One day the old man brought in a recording of Béla Bartók's string quartets performed by The Végh Quartet. In one awful, perfectly choreographed and grinding groan, an expression of communal protest arose from the snot-nosed throng, but ignoring this, our leader removed one vinyl disk from its sleeve and placed it on the turntable.

From the moment the needle hit the groove and music started to pour out of the speakers of the school's dismal little record player, the world as I knew it was forever upended.

Everyone in the room was instantly rendered mute, entranced, transfixed, spellbound. It was as if a new, previously unknown form of life had made its presence known to all of us.

The composition was a canon and the melodies seemed to be spiraling out of the speakers. One after the other, these gorgeous, diaphanous forms gracefully traced and intertwined with each other, winding slowly around the room. They followed one another with utter abandon and yet, such solemnity.

The melodies were alien, atonal, haunting, and utterly beautiful. They had colors, forms. And surely, I was hallucinating—I felt I was actually "seeing" the sound. Or was I perceiving it by some sensory means other than auditory? This music was physically present in the room with all of us. I could kind of see it in front of me and in my mind's eye. The sensation was so unfamiliar I wasn't exactly sure which of my senses were being employed— or violated—by the experience.

Whatever was happening was impossible to measure or describe by any means I had ever known. I glanced around at my slack-jawed classmates and wondered if they were having a similar experience. Was it lost on them that this experience was thousands of times better than getting lit up at the bandshell?

In a moment of realization, I became aware that my own awareness of this Bartók string quartet reminded me of the cartoon vapor trails in old Bugs Bunny cartoons that ensnare and magically transport their victims to a pot of porridge or a slice of pie fresh out of an oven. These vapor trails are characters in their own way—they behave like people with personalities and even have their own uniquely seductive musical themes.

When you think about it, perhaps all sensory stimuli possess some kind of personality trait. As I experienced this Bartók string quartet in that dingy classroom, it seemed that the trails of music that I perceived were revealing their personality to me and to anyone else who was open to the possibility.

How do you perceive sound? Do you just hear it as an event that is generated from a sound source? Or can you also "see" it? Can you identify it with other senses, perhaps as a smell or even a language?

My experience of sound is generally twofold. I perceive it first as a sonic event that is heard and emanates from a specific point of origin, and second, as a nonspecific image or impression that I see in my mind's eye, as opposed to being seen by the sensory equipment designated for sight. They manifest as dark or light forms, occasionally shades of gray, and are nonspecific forms, not familiar objects. These impressions tend to be grainy black and white. I don't ever experience them as colors.

Shapes and shades are relative to sounds and frequencies. When I listen to music and I perceive dark shapes with well-defined outlines, these are generally low-frequency instruments with a great deal of presence. If I perceive a light/white thin shape with well-defined outlines, this can be someone's voice. The sharp outlines are the bite and presence of a sound. If I perceive broad areas that are combinations of gray spots modulated with black and white (which makes a graininess), this can be a distorted electric guitar.

If there are many spots of varying shade or texture, there is more grain to the sound. If the images are smoother or shinier, the sound is smoother and more refined. Often, a bright image also corresponds to notch filtering or phase anomalies, which might be induced by placing multiple microphones on an electric guitar amplifier.

When a sound (or sound field) appears to be either too gray or is too poorly outlined, it is lacking in definition. Sometimes I will see the same image when I'm listening to a low-frequency sound being amplified by a soft-sounding tube amplifier. A transistorized bass amplifier might have a darker, denser image.

The same can be said for "seeing" a similar type of pattern when I encounter another person. It tells me a lot about them. I may see brightness, an even texture, or there may be something vague or unclear about them—perhaps something hidden—a possible motivation or agenda. Sounds are forms of energy—and perhaps in this way, they are similar to people.

Sometimes these images will merge into one another. This also means to me that they are probably poorly defined. I can see when sounds don't balance together properly—for example, the way a specific low-frequency sound might not work well with other sounds or sounds in the same frequency range.

When there is a good sonic/tonal/textural balance, I get a pleasing sensation from the image I'm seeing and I can sense that things are working properly. This isn't based on a preconceived idea or something I thought up—it simply is.

It also provides a palpable, sensory-based point of reference for me to work from. No matter how far away from this reference I go, I can always recall what the image attached to the sound looked like and how it made me feel.

I have always been under the impression that many people experience sound much the way I do. Although most people feel that they do not experience sound beyond the auditory/emotional experience normally attributed to it, they actually do have a multisensory relationship with sound.

What about you? How do you perceive sound?

21

SUPPLEMENTAL ACTIVITIES

My experience is that having at least one supplemental activity outside of your chosen field of endeavor is really healthy. This helps you to maintain your creative flexibility and keep a fresh perspective on your work. Any supplemental activity should do the following:

- Stimulate the intuitive senses
- Stimulate the pathway to the unconscious mind
- Free up emotions that may be clogging up the conscious or subconscious
- Help one think and act outside of their box
- Help one perform activities that don't have a specific purpose or end result and that can be enjoyable as well as stimulating

It's both useful and fun to seek out and experience forms of art that bear no relationship to your chosen art form. This can be a medium of which you have absolutely no understanding but find aesthetically pleasing or get a good feeling from.

It is also helpful to keep a handwritten journal. This journal can contain anything pertinent, ranging from how you are feeling each day to stream-of-consciousness ramblings. By journaling, you are not only able to satisfy your need to be expressive in a different medium, but you can also clear the accumulated sensory experiences of the day out of your head. As these events and experiences accumulate, they can often adversely affect your creativity by bogging it down.

Through writing by hand, one gets the direct interface of thoughts to nerves to hand to writing instrument to paper. It is a direct feedback loop and much different from using a computer.

The author William S. Burroughs addressed the concept of supplemental activities in Daniel Odier's book *The Job: Interviews with William S. Burroughs* when he said, "The point is to apply what we have learned from one discipline to another and not get stuck in one way of doing things."

22

FREE YOURSELF
FROM THE NEED FOR
AN EXPECTED OUTCOME

I love modular synthesizers for so many reasons. They stimulate my intuitive awareness. They are tactile and completely interactive. The sonic possibilities are limitless and the slightest shift of a dial can completely alter the character of a sound. And they look cool. If you're a gearhead, few thrills in life are better than looking at a wall of knobs and cables.

Modular synthesizers were originally designed to be non-tempered instruments—my understanding is that the keyboard was added as an afterthought. By the way, I love that none of my modular systems have keyboards.

While I'm no whiz, I can operate a modular synthesizer without thinking too hard about it. I know what each module does and can fake my way around the rest, but when I sit down in front of one, I have only a general idea of what I'm going to do with it or where I may wind up. I might start playing around with a specific idea in mind but will often find myself going down a completely different path. I am never absolutely certain of the end result. This underscores a valuable lesson—the importance, in any endeavor, of divorcing one's self from the outcome.

By not expecting or relying on a specific or desired outcome and not incorporating this awareness into one's work, it becomes much easier to think outside of the box. Working this way, one is far more likely to take chances instead of trying to play it safe. It also divorces one from simply performing an activity, and instead transforms the activity into a means of letting go—of everything. Performing any act becomes a lesson about the value of process and becoming completely free. Not feeling the need (or the pressure) to have to deliver or present anything specific to someone else makes it easier to follow your heart exactly where it beckons you to go.

Once the pressure and the desperate need to produce a specific result are removed, an entirely new sense, a new awareness, replaces it. The pressure of needing to be a functional part of society is replaced by a sense of true purpose—a sense of true identity. For the first time you are able to access your intent and see how you really appear. Your work becomes a perfect mirror of who you are. And this is where true action begins.

This sensibility can be applied to everything. The fear of failure, the fear of losing, the fear of being rejected, the fear of not being good enough—all are replaced by a sense of wonder and awe for the marvel of creativity; just how easy and joyous it is to simply be creative.

WHAT INSPIRES YOU?

What is inspiring to you? What motivates you to move, to act with intent and clarity (or sometimes in a blind frenzy) in order to expunge and express the emotions that are percolating within your body? What motivates you to express your creative urges?

Often, the creations of others through various media and art forms that they have used to express themselves similarly inspire us to be creative. One may see a remarkable painting and become driven to paint. One may hear a stunning piece of music and be intensely motivated to learn to play an instrument.

Occasionally, people are also inspired to create something new by transmuting elements in their environment into a creative medium, things that pervade their everyday lives.

As an example, Olivier Messiaen composed a piece of piano music called *Catalogue d'oiseaux* which is based on birdcalls that he heard in his garden. Kraftwerk (and other German bands who came from the same music scene) created a driving, repetitious, and rhythmic musical style that was inspired by growing up in close proximity to the heavy industry and machinery that was used to rebuild postwar Dusseldorf.

There are countless stories of musicians, composers, artists, writers, and others who were inspired by various and diverse elements in their immediate environments. Growing up around cities, factories, airports, or farms, or encountering them regularly at important periods in their lives, provided these individuals with priceless opportunities to express themselves creatively and uniquely. To a fertile mind seeking a creative outlet, anything can be turned into inspiration or a tool for creation. The fact is, the entire world (and everything in it) can be perceived as a means and a resource from which one can derive inspiration (or spare parts).

Ambient, environmental sights, sounds, and experiences can be completely removed from their existing context and used accordingly as grist for the artistic mill.

One way to achieve this is to look for a specific type of order within the chaos of a commonplace event in one's immediate environment. For example, a person may walk past a construction site and hear nothing but irritating noise. Another person will encounter this experience in a completely different way. He may hear the rhythmic cadence of a piece of machinery. He may hear the tonal quality of this machinery, how its sonic qualities juxtapose with the sonic qualities of other pieces of machinery or other ambient events that are simultaneously occurring in the same vicinity or time. He may become aware of how these events are naturally orchestrated against one another as percussive instruments (no matter how atonal, noisy, or loud they might be). He may even imagine a melodic event played by some imaginary instrument that decorates and embellishes the machinery at the construction site. He may hear a veritable symphony of noise instead of a construction site.

I was always incredibly inspired by how beautiful and inspiring random elements in my immediate environment were. Back in the early 1980s I found myself on a bus rambling through Lower Manhattan. I began to notice that whenever the bus stopped and began to idle, the engine started vibrating at a sub-bass frequency. The vibrating engine caused the entire bus to vibrate so intensely that my eyes felt like they were jiggling rhythmically in my head.

The vibration also caused the seats at the rear of the bus to shake and rattle, making a loud, metallic squeaking sound. The bus must have been poorly maintained because the bolts that fastened the seats into place were gradually coming loose and the engine sounded like it was in serious trouble.

What interested me was how the seats were squeaking in time with the engine as it growled and thumped. Since the seats were being shaken back and forth so quickly, their squeaking was very punctuated. This perfectly accentuated the rhythm it made and timed it perfectly to the rhythm of the engine vibrating.

I quickly realized that the rhythm of vibrating bus engine and the squeaking sounded exactly like an industrial electro-disco record, with the engine functioning as a driving bass drum/bass rhythm and the seats as hi-hats. The bus was playing a four-on-the-floor beat with accented sixteenth notes. Bus disco. Crazy!

It felt as if the bus was putting on a little show just for me. All I could think of was how it sucked that I didn't have a tape recorder.

Look around you. Open your eyes, open your ears, and listen to what is happening at this very moment. You may not hear the swelling of a fantastic melody in your head, but there may be a thousand other things taking place around you that can be incredibly inspiring if you open yourself to the possibility.

Instead of ignoring the events in your environment as being no more than interference or noise, imagine how it would feel if you experienced them as being inspirational.

What might happen if you were to stop shutting these things out this very instant and let them speak to you? Listen to the tone and regularity of an air hammer as it thuds into the earth. Hear the texture and grain in a jet engine as it tears through the air hundreds of feet overhead. Listen to the echoes of an emergency vehicle siren as the sound caroms off the tall buildings in a city and gradually trails off into the cacophony from which it was born. Experience the multiple musical tones that emanate from some nameless generator in some nameless building performing some nameless function.

How often do we take these things we see around us every day for granted? How often do we miss a spectacular, priceless, unrepeatable moment in time because we are too preoccupied and concerned with what we expect this moment to be—*because we are more obsessed with getting than with receiving?*

With this in mind, now ask yourself how much you take for granted about the creative work you do? How much of the detail, how much of the meaning in it are you missing?

What can you learn from the noise of traffic, the sound of a building being built, the rhythm of a helicopter's wings beating the air just overhead? What might happen if you go into the world right now and experience everything with this brand-new awareness—this heightened perception? What might happen if you were to surrender to this different experience of being alive instead of hearing and seeing the same things, the same way over and over again?

Will it be a waste of time—or will it be life changing? The choice is yours.

23

IDLING DOWN

dling down is an absolutely necessary component in the creative process. It is beneficial to recognize when one's internal engine is weakening and may need to idle for a little while.

In many aspects of life, there is a prevalent misconception that in order to achieve success, people must be absolutely driven to the point of cutting other things out of their lives and working far beyond the point of physical pain.

However, this is only true when people are driven to act in such a way because they are incapable of doing anything else. For those who consciously apply this approach to their work, it is an utter waste of time.

You can't force ambition and you don't want to let ambition force you. You are truly driven only if the drive comes naturally, and then, only to the degree that feels natural. If you are driven by an addiction or a deep psychological need to be recognized, or by the need to avoid other emotions or to make money, your achievements and victories will be largely Pyrrhic and hollow.

It is therefore vitally important to recognize the exact point where your natural drive becomes an excuse to avoid other things that help you balance your life. It is also important to recognize that not everyone is built with the same capacity for ambition. Of course, some people are capable of working themselves literally into the ground. Whether this is an addictive personality trait or the behavior of one who is in constant communion with his creative source is not for anyone else to judge.

What is clear is that most people believe they must keep working past the point where they are capable of producing anything worthwhile. By working this way, they are actually working less efficiently. In fact, they are negatively affecting the overall quality of their work, and, in the long run, making more work for themselves.

This is one reason why it is so important to idle down. You are simply recognizing the fact that you are a human being with unique needs. There is no shame in accepting this.

Due to societal conditioning, many people see making such acknowledgements as a sign of weakness. Actually, such an acknowledgment is a sign of personal strength. It is the recognition of our inner sensitivity—we are opening a deeper connection to our creative sensitivity.

The truth is, we all require replenishment, no matter what our tolerance, our personal abilities, or our endurance. Idling down may have a different meaning for each person. In some cases, it will be little more than going for a massage, a nice meal, or a movie. In other cases, it will mean a complete shutting down of a person's life, to the extent that the individual removes himself or herself completely from everything for a period of time.

24

INTENT

don't hear the hit!"

On numerous occasions, in a misguided attempt to guide them back to the flock, I have heard A&R people make this comment to errant artists who have seemingly lost the plot.

Record business people say things like this because they believe that an artist can pull a rabbit out of his hat on cue, dazzling the world and making everyone who is financially connected to that artist instantly wealthy. It's not hard to surmise from this that many A&R people don't understand artists.

Once you've heard it enough times, you can see through the statement "I don't hear the hit" and understand it for what it truly is—a non sequitur. And by its nature, it shuts its recipient down instead of making him think. It is deflating, uninspiring, and counterproductive. It's the kind of thing you say to people when they aren't doing what you want them to do but you are incapable of explaining to them what you want them to do or how they might do it. It's a prototypical passive-aggressive statement.

The truth is, no one really knows how to write a guaranteed hit song—not even people who get paid handsomely to do so. If they could, you can bet that every song they write would be a hit. Similarly, an A&R person often doesn't understand that an artist's job is to be extraordinary at expressing himself. He doesn't have any idea how to help this artist do his best work. Generally, he is more concerned with keeping his job.

An A&R person is like anyone else with a job, except that his is at a record company. His job revolves around music and, hence, he is expected to have some expertise in how it's made and how to work with the artists who make it.

However, because he is like anyone else with a job (and, in this case, someone who knows nothing about music), he only knows what a hit song sounds like—and how it makes him feel. The A&R person will try to explain what he wants from an artist, but since he often has no idea how to construct a musical idea, he is generally limited to using the work of others as examples to explain what he wants.

Most artists, on the other hand, often have no conception of how to create a hit song, even if they have somehow made one previously—even if one is dropped in their lap with a detailed road map of how to imitate it. An artist is an imperfect machine and can't always imitate something that doesn't come from within him, nor can he replicate something just because he did it once before. He consequently becomes confused because his intuition doesn't necessarily agree with what the A&R person wants. And this is where a disconnect occurs.

Now, imagine if an A&R person listened to an artist's song and—instead of saying, "I don't hear *the hit*"—said to him, "I don't hear *your intent.*" A hit is something tangible (or, at least is a tangible code word) that everyone in the music industry is supposed to understand. But intent? How can you hear that? What is he talking about?

Instead of dropping a confusing non sequitur in the artist's lap, revising the comment to address what his intent is provides him with a positive challenge whereby he can assess his creative process. It directs the artist to the realm of his feelings instead of to the realm of conformity and emulation. It also places the A&R person in the position of having to explain exactly what he means.

While this comment may cause the artist to feel defenseless, the A&R person has the opportunity to recognize the artist's vulnerability and use it to help integrate the artist, to help the artist navigate through the exchange between them instead of leaving him adrift. This opens the door to an honest exchange of dialogue between the two individuals, and their relationship can assume a mutually beneficial aspect.

Helping the artist to focus on the intent behind his work is more beneficial to him than to recommend he emulate something someone else has already done. If *mindfulness* is the state of being, then *intent* is the force that moves being into action. For an artist, following his intent simply means he is present and available to express himself as he feels intuitively driven.

Intent is kind of like the mission statement that accompanies your actions. It is what ultimately comes thorough everything you do and is loudest when it is a genuine expression of your true feelings. Do you ever wonder whether your love for what you do has motivated you to do it, or if you have an agenda that contradicts your intent?

An artist's intent provides him with clarity when others attempt to interpret, alter, or extrapolate his work. Intent is like a bookmark that the artist can reference if he loses his way, or feels uncomfortable about what someone else is doing with his ideas.

Like the artist's state of being, intent simply *is*.

Since an artist's intent is not a conscious product of his mind, neither it nor his talent is truly his property. Instead, he is their guardian—their caretaker. For this reason, he must be committed to ensuring that his work is presented in its purest state and is altered only for the benefit of the work itself.

To observe an example of an artist exercising intent in his creative process, I recommend watching *The Promise*, a documentary from 2010 directed by Thom Zimny, about the making of Bruce Springsteen's album *Darkness on the Edge of Town*. I loved watching the intensity with which Springsteen applies himself to the development and recording of his ideas. It is also amazing how clear he is in his intent and how he permits absolutely no one to divert him when he has made his mind up.

Watching Springsteen's process, you can clearly see the big difference between clear intent and stubbornness. Stubbornness is generated and enacted from ego; clear intent is generated and enacted from personal integrity and truth.

25

IDENTITY

Walk over to a mirror, look into it, and ask your reflection, "Who are you?" Ponder this question for a little while as you stare at yourself. Get lost in the features of your face, and they may slowly begin to morph into those of someone completely unfamiliar to you.

Who are you? What is your intent? What is your purpose? What are you doing here? How do you spend your time? Do you love your life? Do you hate your life? Are you enjoying yourself or simply pretending to? What do you stand for?

I was producing a singer-songwriter who had been moderately successful at one point in his life. However, he was still well connected and had the ear of many powerful people in the entertainment industry. As his career gradually began to flicker and die, his management reached out to various nabobs to find some way, any way, to keep him afloat. An assortment of his music was sent around and, shortly, a multitude of responses came back.

One, in particular stands out to me. This respondent, a highly successful captain of the recording industry, as fate would have it, had at an earlier time, been a record producer and engineer himself on many famous records. His thought was that every great front man needs a great sideman. Robert Plant had Jimmy Page, Tom Petty had Mike Campbell, Bono has the Edge, and so on. Surely, this artist would find success—his identity—if he, too, found his magic guitarist, his faithful Sancho Panza.

I was completely stunned when I heard this. I mean, the guy who made this comment was extremely well known and had been down this path many more times than I had. As I understood his logic, the only way this artist could find validation would be standing next to someone else whose radiance would quantify and multiply his own. What the hell was he talking about?

Sure, it's really important—often vital—to have someone to accompany you if you're a singer, but that's what bands are for. The point is that if there's nothing there to begin with—if there's no "you" with something meaningful to say, having Mick Ralphs in the room isn't going to turn you into Paul Rodgers. You can only get to the greatness in you if you are truly in touch with that "you"—your true identity as a person. To do this, you have to be willing to commit yourself completely and accept that the process will be ongoing into perpetuity. By simply deciding that you will be on the path, it will begin spontaneously. All you need to do is to allow it to unfold and not fight it, come what may.

Each day, every day, you are a work in progress.

GETTING INTO CHARACTER, ROLE-PLAYING

Finding your way into an artist's work makes it easier to relate to what they are doing. This requires going beyond simply listening to a song—you must focus yourself and identify the very thing that you find appealing, outstanding, noteworthy, and attention grabbing about it.

This is similar to the way an actor works to perfect a role that he or she will play. She researches and develops her character thoroughly, assumes mannerisms that define the role, and finds any other means necessary to "inhabit the character"; otherwise, she cannot *become* the part.

Most people who make popular music make no attempt to *become*, to *be*, or to *find* themselves in their work. If an artist is not invested in what he does, no one working with him will be able to connect with it, and consequently, neither will anyone else who encounters it. The main reason art fails is if, from its source it is neither believable nor relatable.

Getting into character is an exercise for the artist and the producer. As the artist works to find (and thereby, express) herself through her work, the producer works to find (and thereby, express) himself through a connection to the artist's work.

When I'm working with an artist, I try to achieve this connection in many ways. I look for adjectives and create mental images that I associate with the artist's music. I might watch movies, read books, listen to other music, and so on, to find cues in these sources that are reminiscent to me of the artist's work. I might even try role-play exercises (first with myself, then with the artist) that help me create a personal context with which to relate to the artist's work. And, of course, I'll speak directly with the artist and get her take on her own work.

You can create cities and entire universes when you find your way into the art you're investing yourself in.

And that's important because, like every other kind of job, working in a recording studio can occasionally suck after a while.

This is why it's good to take a moment and consider the space you're working in. Where you work can have a profound effect on what you create, and, honestly, feeling like you're a bacteriological experiment percolating in a petri dish becomes a real drag before too long. I recently produced a recording where the artist had decided to do the entire project in their rehearsal room. When I first opened the door to the space, my heart literally fell into my stomach. The place was a dingy, utterly depressing veritable refuse heap, with all manner of rubble piled from floor to ceiling. A miniscule area had been hollowed out amid the road cases and cables for a beat-up, sad-looking couch, and there was not an inch for a person to think, let alone stand. It took awhile, but we made the space both comfortable and functional.

Also, if cost is no option and you can work anywhere, what factors are really important to you in your work space—technical and otherwise? Acoustically, I have very specific preferences: I like small, dead control rooms with almost no reflections and large, recording areas—also virtually dead, with a frequency response that favors energy in the low frequencies and doesn't amplify high-mid-range instruments, such as cymbals.

Is your work space accommodating, is it a good use of the area, is it soothing and intimate, or is there too much negative space? When you're there, do you feel that it's difficult to concentrate and all the energy is being sucked out of the room? It's relatively easy to redefine the work space by bringing personal items, furniture, and other totems into a recording studio. This gives it a less sterile and more homey atmosphere. It also helps artists feel less self-conscious, more comfortable, and open to being expressive.

I've noticed that finding an ideal environment to work in kind of takes people back to when they were little children and had a rich fantasy life—spending their time in backyard clubhouses or tree houses, or in the "forts" they built in their homes from chairs and pillows.

Anything was possible then—why not now?

It's vitally important for an artist to constantly see his creative process in new and different ways. Anything that introduces that cognitive dissonance we addressed earlier into the creative process also stimulates the imagination and makes the experience more challenging and rewarding. This is where role-play can be helpful. The concept of shifting one's perception of reality is often easy for an artist to grasp, especially since he occasionally will lapse into character in order to perform.

Role-playing relates to imagining one's self in a different environment or state of being from the one the person is currently occupying. For example, a vocalist may be asked to immerse herself in a specific emotion so she can sing with conviction.

As mentioned earlier, one way to do this is to ask her to consider her intent and describe what that looks like. Another is to ask her to visualize what she is singing about and to describe that. If she is singing a song about lost love, can she see and describe the object of her affection, how they parted, what the environment looked like, and where they stood when they said their last good-bye? If she can envision this, she can immerse herself in the imagery and the concomitant emotions they conjure. This makes the experience of the song hyper real and emotional (if she has truly invested herself into it) for the artist.

She can also envision a similar situation that occurred in her life—and call on all her sensory recollections surrounding the event to act as emotional triggers. This is a very powerful way to connect emotionally with a song.

Outside of a recording studio, role-play and recontextualizing your environment are also helpful in broadening the creative experience. This works for me and is often enlightening and fun. Try this: Walk through a familiar landscape, paying close attention to a specific aspect of that environment, such as the various sounds. Tune out everything else and focus on nothing more than the sounds in the environment. Bring a recording device to enhance your focus on this singular aspect.

Did you notice anything different? Did it seem as if your altered perception turned a previously familiar environment into something foreign, yet magical?

Now, pretend you live in a world where cell phones and computers don't exist. Try going for five hours (eight, if you can manage it!) without any of your devices. How long will it take before (a) you feel like you're suffocating, (b) you're going crazy, or (c) you're completely at peace?

Can you survive a full withdrawal and detox from constantly being in touch with the entire world? Does having all those devices feel like a necessity, or an addiction? What if this world was exactly as it is but there were no mobile wireless devices and no computers? What if the only means you had to communicate with people was by talking and directly interacting with them? How does this make you feel?

Pretend that every person you see is a member of your family. How do you see them now? How are you treating them as a result?

Pretend every person you see is nothing more than an extension of yourself, like an arm or a leg. How do you see them now? How are you treating them as a result?

Pretend that you are looking down at every person you see from a very tall building. Everyone looks the same from so high up. They all seem like ants—you could crush any of them whenever you like—and feel nothing. How are you treating them as a result?

Pretend every person you see is a reflection of yourself. How are you treating them as a result?

Pretend you are the wealthiest person in the world, but no one else is allowed to know.

Pretend your emotional state is volatile and you can't control yourself from expressing every feeling that comes up, no matter how outrageous it is.

Pretend you're completely shut down and disassociated emotionally from everything and everyone around you.

How have these exercises affected you? Has anything changed for you perceptually?

SELF-COACHING

Self-coaching is another way to stay mindful and present in your process. You can implement this by giving yourself a daily pep talk, a daily run-through regarding each day's agenda, or a general means of checking in each day.

You can assess your goals over the course of your day, what you need to be aware of (potential pitfalls), and how to avoid confusing the agendas of other people in the creative space with your own.

This is similar to meditation because of its inward focus, and it is ideally done sitting in a quiet, private space. It can be a monologue spoken to yourself (as if you're having a conversation with someone else and advising them); it can also be recorded or written down.

Self-coaching is done by being present in your body and giving complete attention to each aspect that requires attention. By doing this you can establish a road map of intent for your day.

JOURNALING

Years ago, I had a conversation with Brian Eno about techniques for keeping the creative mind open and agile. He said that one of his favorite methods was to keep a journal. He would write about everything that was happening from day to day. He also recorded his dreams. He did this by waking himself up after having a dream and transcribing it while it was still fresh.

As time passes, thoughts and feelings may arise that occupy your mind and make it difficult to focus on your work. When this happens, you may talk to other people about it, but often, talking alone may not address how these feelings are interfering with your creative process. When you write about your experiences in a journal, you can address your feelings on a few different levels. You have complete freedom to write anything you want. You are not engaging with anyone else, and, consequently, you don't have to think about how what you are divulging might be taken by another person, how it might make you look to them, and how they might respond to you as a result.

By journaling, you are simply reporting what is happening to you, what you think about it, and how you feel about it. You may write about something symptomatic ("I'm having trouble focusing on work") and gradually address your emotions ("I feel sad because of family issues").

By converting your emotions into written words, you are also converting them into a constructive process, using them to flex your creative muscles and making them grist for your creative mill.

Journaling is a relative of "automatic writing," which is free-associative expression and can plug a person into his own unconscious. Through writing whatever comes into your mind or your heart (instead of writing *about* something), you're able to delve deep into your unconscious as well as mine your surface emotions.

By spending some time every day journaling, you can break down creative blocks, clear out mental space, and let go of whatever may be troubling you. When you journal, there is also no pressure on you to be anything other than yourself. Journals aren't written to be shared with others nor are they written to be reread or analyzed. You can journal whether you are a terrible writer or a Nobel laureate. It doesn't matter, because you don't journal to look good. You do it to feel good.

MENTORING, OR "I GOT MINE, YOU GET YOURS"

I have a friend who has enjoyed a lengthy and legendary career in the music industry. He's worn every hat from that of artist to manager to record company executive, and also, one of the best record producers ever. After not having spoken for several years, we recently met for lunch.

I have always considered this individual a kindred spirit and was anticipating a stimulating conversation. Dispensing quickly with pleasantries, we began discussing the state of popular music and related elements in its periphery.

It quickly became obvious that in every possible way, we were on completely different wavelengths.

One major point of contention between us was the concept of mentoring. While I feel that people like us with a wealth of experience have a duty to mentor others, this guy had an entirely different perspective. He insisted that the new generation of performers don't need help—mine, his, or anyone else's. His point of view seemed somewhat Darwinian (or, perhaps, Ayn

Rand-ian): the artists of this new generation should be left to their own devices and find their own way. After all, we had found ours, and look how we turned out.

Although this last statement is partially true, it's also important to consider that the world he and I had grown up in was much different from the one we currently inhabit. Back then (and until fairly recently), if you worked in a creative field and were ambitious and talented enough, it wasn't uncommon to eventually find yourself under the wing of a mentor. From there, the synergy from your interaction with this mentor could help you attain the heights that you sought. I, myself, didn't have one specific guy who mentored me when I was starting out. However, I kept meeting these old-school characters with extraordinary experiences and wild stories, and I kept learning more and more that every one of us were components in an amazing continuum of artists that spanned back over eons. This made me feel special—as though I, too, were part of something much bigger than anything I could comprehend. Plus, the stories I heard were amazing.

Sometimes a mentor would share his knowledge with you, introduce you to his connections, or thrust you into a frightening situation (such as being told to run a recording session out of the blue), which was actually a rite of passage to put you on the path to becoming a great artist. Sometimes you'd find yourself in a mentor's presence while he worked and you'd watch everything he did, and incorporate it into your own workflow.

At that time, people took art and artists a little more seriously, and if you were really good, there was an unspoken support system in place readily available to carry you along. A new talent who could potentially do great things in the future was seen as an asset to the entire community he or she worked in. There was that awareness of a continuum, and helping someone else was part of it.

In every business, people seek out mentors who will instruct them and show them the proverbial "ropes." There isn't a single person I know who achieved remarkable things without the help of a mentor at some stage in his life. When it comes to making or recording music, this is no longer the case.

We are now in what is being called a DIY age. And, as my friend kept insisting, the younger generation will figure everything out on their own—the same as we did. However—unlike us—they don't appear to need mentors.

That's because this generation has a leg up—something we didn't have when we were finding our way. They have the Internet. You can find any information about anything on the Internet. If you want to learn how to use an acetylene torch, go on the Internet. If you want to know why your tongue has gone numb and turned bright green, go on the Internet. And, if you want to learn how to operate a DAW, you can go on the Internet.

The ability we have to find the information we seek is unprecedented. In fact, there's almost too much of it—with no adulteration or filtration. With all this information floating around, who needs education? Who needs schools? And who needs mentors?

Alvin Toffler popularized the term *information overload* in his book *Future Shock*. This refers to the difficulty people have processing ideas when there is too much information accompanying these ideas. When Toffler concocted this term, I wonder if he also imagined the numbing effect that information overload would have on its victims.

Karl Marx said that religion is the opiate of the masses. Horace Mann said that education is the great equalizer of men.

Information has become the new religion of today and free access to information has begun to supersede education as the way people learn things. If you mash up Mann and Marx's quotes, they could be contemporized thus: *Information is the great equalizing opiate of the masses.* In a sense, information is becoming the junk entertainment of this era—useless, served up in bulk, and, essentially, a narcotic masquerading as something of substance.

One significant thing that separates the acquisition of information from the Internet from the experience of being mentored (apart from the fact that a lot of Internet information is neither verified nor accurate) is that mentoring is a direct, highly personal experience, offered by a master.

A mentor gets to know his apprentice personally, uses his intuition to sense what the apprentice needs, and helps the apprentice develop his own skills. The personalized one-on-one experience of mentoring has nothing to do with doing a Google search or sitting in a recording academy classroom with twenty other people whose ambition it is to pull down major bucks by mixing big-budget pop records so they can own a canary yellow Bentley GT Coupe and a mansion in the Pacific Palisades.

The mentoring process is unique because it involves the transmission of something both sacred and immensely valuable from a mentor to his apprentice—the mentor's own physical reactions to his own experiences. Without a human connection, dispensing and accumulating knowledge is just a dry activity with no meaning or purpose.

Centuries ago, people apprenticed through trade guilds or would seek out a master to teach them a trade. The primary benefits of this system were on-the-job training and personalized transmission of practical knowledge from an expert. This is how knowledge has been passed from teacher to student for generations. It's also how many great engineers and producers learned their skills.

The annals of recording lore are rife with stories of "tape-ops" and "tea boys" being taken under the wing of a legendary producer who saw a spark of greatness in them. Many of them would become assistants, continuously demonstrating their worth while gradually moving up through the ranks under the tutelage of their mentor. And one day, the assistant would show up for a random session and the producer would tell him that he was driving.

Without any preparation, the kid is suddenly running the show. And he had better be on point because there will be no second chances. Talk about being dropped into the deep end of the pool. Needless to say, there is no school that teaches this, but it's the only way to learn.

Back at lunch, I was more than a little stunned by my friend's attitude and asked him if, as a creative individual, he had absolutely no desire to share his limitless knowledge and experience with young people who could really benefit from it. His response was that if anyone wanted his advice, they'd have to ask for it.

I'm sure that the people who mentored my friend back when he was coming up (and there were more than a few) were rolling vigorously around in their graves at that instant. Of course, I understood why my friend was so reticent to share his wisdom. Being a mentor is both time- and effort-intensive, and, as we have all heard too often, time is money.

Sadly, his attitude underscores a tremendous problem in contemporary society and is summed up by the timeworn saying "I got mine, you get yours." Anyone who looks at life in this way wants you to know that nothing in this world is free. They want you to know that they had to work hard to get what they have, and now that they've got it, if you want some, you'll have to pay for it, just like they did.

People also have their so-called value (or conversely, what they think they're worth). In our society, the value of a person is no longer measured by his or her ethics, demeanor, or good works. It has instead become a pejorative measurement, determined by physical appearance, the ability to accumulate material wealth, and celebrity. And everything must cost something. These are all surface elements and are all about status.

Status—position, wealth, and so on, have been fixtures in civilizations dating back thousands of years, but in this civilization, these elements have eclipsed virtually everything else.

This is the age of the entrepreneur, and everyone is expected to be one. Every waking moment contains within it the seed for a moneymaking scheme that will somehow make the hopeful entrepreneur wealthy beyond measure. From credit-card telemarketing, to IPOs for up-and-coming tech companies nobody ever heard of, to playing the lottery, to inane and profligate cases of litigation, there are a thousand and one ways to get rich quick.

And now that everyone the whole world over is expected to be an entrepreneur and to become a "brand," people generally don't feel comfortable doing anything unless they know what's in it for them.

Times are hard, people say. I have to make the payment on my Mercedes S600 V12 sedan. I have needs. I gotta get paid. I worked hard for all this. What have you done for me lately?

I got mine. You get yours.

Nowadays, working for the sheer joy of it is as heretical an idea as the notion of giving your time for something absurd like mentoring people without being paid. "What—enjoy what I do? I don't do this because I enjoy it. What are you, some kind of communist?"

I am a baby boomer and I feel the buck stops with my generation. We are the ones who have gradually decimated the cultural imperative to mentor others. We have replaced it with a new prevailing wisdom that is, if you give of yourself and you don't receive an equivalent quantity of money as compensation for what you are giving (based on whatever the current market rate happens to be), you are either cheating yourself or you are being taken advantage of.

In either case, you are a sucker.

The thing is, when knowledge is passed from a teacher to a student, there is always an exchange that takes place. There are no suckers and everyone wins.

This is because the knowledge a mentor possesses is meant for her to share, not hold on to. There are others in the world to whom this knowledge is also meant to go, and sharing it not only establishes a new link in the continuum but also settles the original bill for that knowledge. This bill was established the moment the mentor received her education from whoever mentored her. The debt incurred is resolved by paying it forward in the same way the mentor first received it—to someone worthy and diligent. In a sense, this process is like doing community service or teaching at a specialized trade school, where your compensation is what you already received when you were starting out, all those years ago. This is also a wonderful experience for the mentor; it offers her a deeper understanding about what she does and how better to share it.

Having mastery of something is marvelous, but having the ability to share that mastery with others is a blessing. Through mentoring others, a master becomes a teacher. Teaching and the transmission of knowledge is a sacred trust and imbues one with a sense of purpose. Within this sense of purpose, one discovers meaning and true value—things that are far different from the monetary value of a commodity that one can buy or sell.

IS IT REALLY WORTH THE EFFORT TO BECOME GREAT?

If you can muster the attention span, watch an orchestra perform sometime. You might learn something. As you're listening, pay attention to the string section. Then, focus on the trombones. What do these instruments have in common? They have no frets, no keys, and no valves. They are nontempered, which means that there are no note indicators or tuned keys that can be used so these instruments can be played in pitch. If a musician wants to play a violin in pitch, he has to know how to find the pitch on the instrument.

Next, look at some of the other instruments in the brass section: trumpet, French horn, and tuba. Notice that they generally have three valves. In spite of this, someone playing a brass instrument must somehow get a few octaves' worth of 12-note scales out of it. This is mainly done with a combination of those three valves and minute changes in the player's embouchure, or the lip position he uses to make sound come out. Did I mention that developing an embouchure is an art form in itself?

And somehow, with all the headaches that come with learning how to play nontempered instruments and instruments with only a few valves on them, quite a few wacky individuals have chosen to do just that. They not only learn how to play these instruments in discrete 12-tone scales (or many more if you're playing Arabic music), entire orchestras are formed incorporating large groups of other wacky people who spent a good deal of their lives doing the exact same thing.

And while you might find the end result of their efforts tedious, time wasting, and too challenging to your attention span, consider the effort it takes to first play one of these instruments in pitch, then to get good at it, and, eventually, to get so good you get to perform with other elite musicians in a symphony orchestra. Now, consider that all this effort goes into replicating music that has been in existence for hundreds of years and will likely be known for hundreds of years in the future.

It takes a superhuman amount of effort and talent to be good at something. It requires effort and talent far beyond human comprehension to be truly great.

Being in a rock band is very easy by comparison to being a cellist. Your instrument either emanates from your mouth, or has frets or keys, or you hit stuff. Not much of a stretch there. And you can teach yourself how to do it, if that's your pleasure.

That's what I did. I bought a synthesizer when I was fourteen. I barely knew music, didn't have a clue what I was doing with the synth. But I learned. At first it sounded like crap. After many years, it began to turn into something.

Not long ago, a friend sent me a link to an interesting website. The substance of this site summed up thousands of years of musical evolution—how people went from making music by beating on logs to learning how to play violins and trombones all the way to the sophistry of moving a cursor around on a computer screen to create a dance track.

In its "about us" mission statement, the company (whose name won't be mentioned for obvious reasons) states definitively that absolutely anyone can forgo years of experience and become a fabulous pop music superstar (or, at very least, simulate one) in an instant by using their patented algorithm. This algorithm will help you create a piece of "music," provide you with prefabricated beats and instrument parts that represent a variety of pop styles, and record/tune your vocals for a finished track worthy of the *Billboard* Hot 100.

This is what it's come to. Millennia of various musical traditions—all distilled down to this unique moment in time when some random person has a hankering to imitate a Katy Perry song with a just few keystrokes on their Mac, pays an admission fee, and just like that—attains immediate gratification. Who said progress wasn't wonderful?

However, it's not progress that's at issue here. It actually starts with the casual disdain with which music itself has been treated by the music business. This lack of respect has gradually trickled down to the greater listening public, which is now effectively convinced that music is nothing more than a commodity—like a pair of shoes or a backpack. Because of the ubiquity of the product, as well as the facility and the readily available technology to make it, music has lost much of its cache and its cultural importance.

Over the past few decades, popular music has gone through a dramatic transmogrification. If you think about it, this shape shifting has paralleled the life cycle of most baby boomers. Over the transition of the 1950s to the 1960s, popular music transformed from a force for adolescent rebellion to a force for societal change. From there, it became a source of great revenue and was representative of a hedonistic lifestyle in the 1970s. In the late

'70s and early 1980s, music became momentarily rebellious again, immediately thereafter sprouting gargantuan shoulder pads and a nasty cocaine addiction.

A few stints in rehab later, the 1990s rolled around, popular music wised up, cleaned up, and generated multiple income streams while still courting artists and falling off the wagon a couple more times. As the income streams grew steadily, it became clearer that popular music couldn't sustain all that hard work forever. It had lost its idealism somewhere around the ass-end of punk rock in the early '80s and gradually developed a longing to own that grotesquely large, yet somehow austere, Edwardian mansion in Westchester that it had been eyeing for years.

It began to think more and more about retirement and living off its Roth IRA, 401(k), and mutual funds. It was time for a quiet, sedentary life laden with dividends, triannual trips to Europe, and grandchildren spastically racing across vast, finely manicured lawns fitted with computer-controlled sprinkler systems.

And, as those baby boomers became so jaded and so quick to sell out their faith in the music that had been both soundtrack and fuel to their lives, their attitudes also leached into the general public. The irony is that the bloated, used-up old men who are trying to hold the fractured shell of the music business together with duct tape and their own spit were once starry-eyed dreamers who had been moved to the depths of their souls by the spirit of music and the promise of what it could offer everyone in the world.

But eventually you get old, the blinders of idealism come off, and you don't feel like working as hard as you once did. Maybe you're just worn out, or maybe you're just tired of watching other people in the same racket making billions instead of millions. And when your life has gradually become all about *taking* instead of *giving*, a weird vortex is set into motion. When a few people in a crowd decide they're going to get what they're entitled to and to hell with everyone else, everyone else in their vicinity is instantly compelled to do the same thing. Somehow, conformity always seems to wind up with a mob.

And now, a handful of venture capitalists and ex–music business people who have been feverishly racking their collective brain pool every possible way to cash in one more time as the music business collapses around them into dust, are offering their solution to the problem. However, their solution completely diverts our attention away from real talent, real effort, and the notion of real commitment to an art form.

Still, what if they're right? Perhaps this company—with its website, canned beats, and music algorithms—is the face of progress. The old ways and forms are being paved over and programmed out of existence to make way for the new. And perhaps, that's the way God and nature intends it. Or perhaps we're just in the eye of the storm and can't see the forest for the trees. Yet.

I feel that it's a little too easy and a little too soon to give up on virtues such as talent, effort, and commitment, and on ideals such as greatness, especially not in favor of conformism and mediocrity. As long as there is someone, somewhere, who yearns to experience greatness by way of prodigious expressive talent, there need to be artists who will provide that greatness.

Perhaps this is one reason that artists aspire to greatness, even in the most extreme and seemingly inane and pointless ways. To counterbalance all the mediocrity in the world.

26

THE BLIND TERROR
OF PERFORMANCE

Over time, I've noticed that more than a few artists I've worked with dislike performing. This is especially the case with vocalists. You can see it in their demeanor, how they carry themselves, how they instantly freeze up when they enter a recording studio. They become apprehensive, and when they smile, it feels forced. Some drink a lot of alcohol prior to singing, or take meds to cut their anxiety. Sometimes, they even get so anxious prior to singing that they become nauseous and occasionally vomit.

I've often found myself wondering why some singers had to virtually be dragged kicking and screaming into their own recording sessions. Why was it the vocalist (more than the other band members) who mysteriously became deathly ill a day or so before he or she had to begin singing? Why, after receiving numerous requests to avoid alcohol, was it the singer who'd go out and get drunk the very evening before an important vocal session?

Why did the vocalist so often manage to piss off and disappoint the rest of the band, who were forced to sit around and twiddle their thumbs waiting for him to finish his work long after they'd finished theirs?

Are vocalists the result of a genetic mutation that relieves its host of impulse control?

Do vocalists somehow will illness, pestilence, and unspeakably bad timing upon themselves? Are they actually demigods, with the powers of life, death, and schedule-obliteration at their beck and call?

To be fair, not all singers are like this. Many are highly professional and often the dominant personalities on a recording session.

Years ago, I worked with a vocalist who was very open about his deep dislike of recording studios. He made it clear that when he wasn't needed, he would be nowhere near any studio while recording was taking place. When his moment to sing eventually arrived, I discovered just how much he despised recording studios and why.

He didn't dislike being in recording studios as much as he disliked the job he had to do when he was in one. To him, being in a recording studio meant hard work, responsibility, and being scrutinized. That is exactly what he was attempting to avoid. Even lounging in a recording studio doing absolutely nothing invoked a deep sense of dread in him.

Over time, he'd gradually built up a negative association with recording and studios. Because he was so terrified by the experience, the only way he could get psyched enough to sing was to wind himself up and become incredibly anxious. We'd start recording him and often, he would become so tense after a few passes that he would start yelling at the engineer and at me. We began to fear having any kind of verbal interaction with him while the recording was taking place, as this would almost always turn unpleasant.

Each day, when he finished singing, instead of asking to listen to what he'd done, his only question would be if he was needed further. And the moment he got clearance to leave, he'd be gone from the premises as if he'd been shot from a cannon.

One day he showed up at the studio and announced that his dentist had found an abscess in his jaw. He had to go on a course of antibiotics and this would stop him from working for at least a month. I was grateful for the artist's sake that his dentist had caught this before it potentially erupted into a catastrophe. In spite of that, I also found the timing of this contretemps nothing short of miraculous. As it is often said, there are no accidents.

Singing in a studio had become a dry, joyless experience for this person—something he felt forced to do to support himself and his family. He didn't like the responsibility; he was terrified by the scrutiny and couldn't stand being asked to redo anything he'd recorded.

But his biggest fear was having to pay attention to what he was doing, to focus and apply himself. His workflow was based on getting his job done as quickly as possible; however, it also facilitated him avoiding his feelings and his life. Perhaps he felt he'd suffered enough and he'd earned the right to coast.

Performing in a recording studio meant having to focus and open himself up to the raw, visceral, emotional experience of life. There would be retakes, hard work, and tedium—all things that made this experience unbearable. He'd already done that when he was younger and solved the problem by drowning himself in drugs and alcohol. Having to focus intently on anything had become so foreign to him that it was now abhorrent.

Every time he approached the microphone to sing, I felt him seething with resentment. It was resentment for having to do something as well as he could and having to do it over and over until he got it right. There's a metaphor in that scenario for life itself.

I also felt his blind panic—like that of an animal trying to stay alive. Performance is petrifying. This is true for nearly everyone in some way, but it's generally hardest for vocalists. I think it goes back to how personal singing is; it's the only form of expression exclusively generated in, and transmitted from, the human body. Singing reveals who a person really is.

In fairness, being in the spotlight has upsides and downsides. And when all eyes are on you, you have no choice—you must do your job and do it very well. Singing in a recording studio is a bit like being on a battlefield with a weapon in hand. You get a handful of chances to wield your weapon, and you must use it with skill in order to survive... or else. The scrutiny and the effort of it can rub a person raw. Being examined like a bug in a jar, being analyzed by people whose lips you can see moving through the studio window. Watching people watching you who you've hired to assess you and are obviously talking about you but you don't know what they're saying. Every paranoid bone in your body is being stimulated to the point of snapping. If one word you have sung or one breath is out of place, you have to repeat what you just attempted to do with all the intensity you can muster. Except, next time, you have to do it better and get it right; otherwise, you'll have to do it again.

And every so often, a nagging question pops into your head: could this be the dreaded moment that you come up to the microphone to open your mouth and suddenly... you simply can't anymore?

You have to stay focused, but being a sensitive person, it is easy to occasionally visit the hell of your own mind and fester in your own self-critical, self-denigrating thoughts. Anyway, how can a human being sing perfectly for hours and days on end?

When we started recording vocals on Soundgarden's album *Superunknown*, I noticed that Chris Cornell seemed distracted and uncomfortable when he was singing. Prior to this, I had seen Chris perform live and got the general impression that he had a hard time connecting with the audience. Whenever I saw or thought about Chris performing, the mental image of a cat being stared at while pooping in his litter box would pop into my head.

I did notice that Chris could play every instrument (extremely well), could engineer, and had demoed all his songs at home, by himself.

I decided to try an experiment.

My plan was to have Chris work alone, record as many full passes of vocals per song as he wanted, and then I'd create a composite vocal track. The engineer and I showed him how to operate the recording console and tape machine remote so he could record his vocals. We set his microphone up in a cardioid pattern (which means the microphone primarily picks up sounds that are in front of it, while rejecting sound in the rear), with no headphones and with loudspeakers wired out of phase and aimed at the rear of the microphone.

We got everything working and I asked Chris to come get me when he felt he either had a finished song or he was through for the day. With that, I left him alone to work.

I'll never forget the expression on his face at the end of the first day. He was ecstatic, fulfilled, and relieved. The pressure he had been feeling was off his shoulders and he could truly focus on his singing without being distracted by the presence of other people.

Inevitably, there is a moment for every person when they have to face the things in life they most fear. Quite often, these things are so terrifying that the thought of experiencing them brings out the worst in a person—let alone a performer. Simply accepting this reality makes it easier to face the actual issue head-on. Once it has been dealt with, it becomes clear that the worst part of the experience was anticipating it, whereas, the experience itself was easy by comparison.

Quite often, the experience of performing is a veritable trial by fire, but it can be also be the most life-affirming experience imaginable. As a producer, I feel it is my job to help make the experience as meaningful as possible for the performer so that he can walk away from it feeling transformed and with a renewed sense of purpose.

27

WHAT IS ARTIST DEVELOPMENT?

Now that the music business no longer develops artists, more emphasis has been placed on artists running their own businesses, developing themselves and their own careers.

There is a world of difference between someone with the talent to be a musical artist and someone who is an inspired music fan. Once in a while, a random music fan may acquire the fantastical belief that because he feels so passionately about music, it should also be his calling. He may feel passionately enough to buy an instrument, go to a music school or a recording school and learn a music-related skill, and he may even get good at what he's doing.

However, without real talent, no amount of education, passion, or ambition will cause anyone to be *great*. True greatness comes from within. It is either there from the outset or it isn't.

In spite of this, there is still a need for talent to be developed and to mature, to be allowed to flourish in its natural state while receiving the nourishment necessary to become even greater still. Greatness can only come when development is applied to talent.

Although record companies invented the concept of artist development, they no longer provide development for artists. Now, there are college courses, recording academies, seminars, and online coaches who teach fundamentals of the music business to a great mass of fledgling musical entrepreneurs. You can even find websites where, for $25, an "industry professional" will provide a few paragraphs' worth of analysis and epithets about one of your songs. Even though the revenue streams are evaporating, there are still multitudes of entrepreneurs trying every way they can to monetize "the new music business," as it is now being called.

Many of them do nothing more than convince poor, unsuspecting musicians to do what they are already doing—tour all over creation, try to sell a few thousand CDs and T-shirts out of the back of a van, and slowly build a following from their blood, toil, tears, and sweat. To further facilitate this, experts will instruct bands in the fine art of self-marketing, including tutelage on "branding" and merchandising themselves in the most efficient ways possible. Why, even the record companies have finally jumped on the implementation of this "branding bandwagon" into their own business model.

Nothing is ever said about improving the quality of the music the artist makes. And that, in short, is modern artist development.

Here's a little story to illustrate my point. Not long ago, I dropped by a certain well-known record company to visit an acquaintance and share some of my own ideas about working with artists. We spoke for a while—he was very receptive and suggested we find some developing artists with whom to do test runs.

The next step was for me to meet his A&R staff and from there, some artists. He introduced me to one of his A&R staff members and explained to him what I was proposing. At one point, the term *artist development* came up. A light must have turned on in the A&R guy's head right then, because a split second later he proceeded to bloviate ad infinitum.

"Weeeellllll, you knowwww...," said the A&R guy in his A&R drawl.

Certain A&R people have a unique style of diction, which I refer to as the "A&R drawl." It's a way of speaking that drips from the speaker's lips like a thick, gelatinous slime and begins to congeal the moment it makes contact with the air. It can begin as a monotone note, but gradually diverges into a series of melodic pushes that are clearly meant to evoke the speaker's casual bravado.

A&R drawl is roughly cross-pollinated from the slurry scansion of a Western gunslinger (sans the twang), the slick pitch of a used-car salesman, the dulcet mumble of James Dean, and a beret-wearing, bongo-playing, Wayfarer-sporting Bohemian hipster straight out of out of central casting, clad in formfitting black clothes, who recites his poetry in dark clubs and shoots heroin with his emaciated girlfriend, who he occasionally beats up for fun.

"Weeeellllll, you knowwww...," said the A&R guy in his A&R drawl, "Artist development is one thing that Acme Records excels at. We're at the top of the food chain. *Harrumph*, we get our bands out on the road, *harrumph*, build a fan base, sell T-shirts and CDs out of the back of a van, *harrumph*, radio play, audience awareness, *harrumph*, *harrumph*, *harrumph*."

As I stood there and politely endured each successive statement and *harrumph* from the A&R guy, it became painfully clear that "artist development" meant something entirely different to this person than it did to me.

In the midst of his furious bluster, I couldn't help noticing that he made no mention of such trivialities as songs and song-writing. It occurred to me that some A&R guys appear to have no idea where songs come from (much the same way that small children have no idea where babies come from).

Perhaps they believe that songs magically appear to artists when the stork drops them down a chimney. Or maybe they think songs emerge from the sea fully formed, like Botticelli's Venus. In any case, after they magically appear, these guys apparently presume that the songs magically improve by being played dozens of times in front of live audiences and, in some magical, inexplicable way, the band also improves. And this means that even after more than fifty years, A&R people are still indiscriminately imposing The Beatles-playing-hellholes-in-Hamburg-four-gigs-a-night-eight-days-a-week-for-over-two-years-straight meme on artists as the ironclad means for success.

Which may actually work—if you happen to be as good as the Beatles. Of course, let's not forget, the Beatles becoming great as a band versus the Beatles becoming great as songwriters are two completely separate issues.

While living out of a van for a few years and playing a boat-load of shows can be formative for many bands, it's time to dispel some of the myths and generalities regarding artist development.

At this point, I think it's naïve to hope that record companies will get a clue about artist development, how music is made, and how the creative process works. In spite of this, I'm going to give a few unsolicited doses of common sense to anyone (in a record company or otherwise) who actually does plan on developing artists.

First, tossing your band in a van and sending them on a road trip to nowhere will not a Beatles make. Second, applying arbi-trary formulas to your artist (such as, believing that shipping your band out in a van like a bunch of UPS parcels will transform them into the Beatles) is not artist development. Third, teaching a band about branding themselves is wasteful. Unless the artist has a natural inclination toward self-promotion (and you are A&R'ing the new Jimmy Page—in which case—lucky you), this is a job best left to someone who is really good at it. Otherwise, you've just given a person with an already short attention span veritable carte blanche to focus on something other than what he does best, which is making music.

Finally—you won't get what you want by manipulating artists to sound the way you think they should. However, you can wind up with something even better by seeing what the artist is, and then, figuring out how to make it better.

The truth is, artist development is very simple. Once you really know who the artist is, developing him consists of applying various stimuli to the artist's creative process so that he can reach his full potential. This won't happen quickly and is not a short-term project. It often requires years of dedication and commitment from both the artist and whoever is helping him develop. It also takes a lot of foresight to recognize that an artist has the potential to be developed and envision how far he might go with the right encouragement.

In the past, when an artist was developed, the record company's job would be to provide everything from financial to moral, and often, creative support. Because of their prodigious abilities as scouts and supporters of talent, executives such as John Hammond at Columbia, Ahmet Ertegun at Atlantic, and Jac Holzman at Elektra were essential links in the creative process. Developing an artist meant believing in him—letting him experience failure without cutting him loose, giving him more than one shot at making a record and always supporting his talent.

There is little doubt that without artist development, superstars such as Bruce Springsteen, Bob Dylan, U2, and the Beatles would have never have come to their ultimate fruition.

If you develop an artist, this also means you're in a relationship with him. No relationship between two people can work if it's predicated on one person trying to force the other to be who they want him to be, instead of encouraging him to be who he is.

The underlying premise to artist development is simple: if you don't like who the artist is at his essence, don't get into a relationship with him. If you like the artist, let the relationship proceed from there.

The rest is easy.

28

THE OTHER CREATIVITY CRISIS

About two years ago a friend directed me to an article in *Newsweek* magazine titled "The Creativity Crisis." This article was written by an author named Po Bronson and addressed the gradually dwindling resource of creativity in the United States. As the topic of creativity is near and dear to my heart, I dove into the article with great anticipation. When I was done reading, I found myself fascinated by the scope of information that had been presented.

Within a minute of finishing the article, I felt myself growing agitated by the awareness it had stirred up in me—that there is an obvious lack of attention paid in this country to this incredibly valuable resource, especially when compared to how highly creativity is clearly valued in other countries. The documentation that Bronson had provided was truly sobering.

A few minutes after this feeling subsided, I became irritated by something else. Okay, I was pissed off. This article was fascinating and well written. The author made good points regarding how creativity, creative thinking, and creativity training are largely overlooked in this country, with far greater emphasis placed instead on the mastery of subjects such as math and science, and scoring high on standardized aptitude tests. This article had clearly underscored a serious problem in our country.

In spite of this, I felt the author was also implying something subtextual beyond the central focus of his piece—or, perhaps, excluding it. One element that had caught my attention was how he presented the concept of creativity itself. I thought I detected an agenda within the article that seemed to emanate from a unique, very specific, proacademic, somewhat antiart bias.

At first it seemed confusing and foreign, but gradually I began to realize I'd encountered this attitude before and it was permeating into every level of culture. As it began to sink in, I realized that there was no innuendo in the way this message was being delivered—it was blatant and as plain as day. It spoke to how creativity is now viewed primarily as a commodity—something, like every other facet of life, exclusively meant to provide functionality, not to describe a freeform process of expression.

One line in the article read, "Researchers say creativity should be taken out of the art room and put into homeroom." Another line insisted, "The age-old belief that the arts have a special claim to creativity is unfounded."

After this, the author continued, "When scholars gave creativity tasks to both engineering majors and music majors, their scores laid down on an identical spectrum, with the same high averages and standard deviations. Inside their brains, the same thing was happening, ideas were being generated and evaluated on the fly." What I found noteworthy was that there was no statistical evidence of this testing accompanying these assertions. Where was this testing done, and by whom? Were these creativity tasks regarding new ways to improve productivity in a hypothetical factory producing turbine engines for agriculture, or did they pertain to improving the flow of a piece of visual art in order to give it more emotional resonance?

Whose definition of creativity set the criteria for this alleged testing?

In fact, the author had identified "what the University of Georgia's Mark Runco calls 'art bias'"—the implication being that we have been brainwashed into believing the fanciful notion that exposure to the arts in an educational environment makes people more creative (and, on a deeper level, that art has value and meaning in the modern world). I got the basic drift— he's saying that creativity isn't the exclusive provenance of the arts. However, neither is creativity exclusive to so-called practical endeavors, such as coding, science, or aspiring to be an entrepreneur. The fact is that being an artist has far less societal acceptance (or even cache) than does being a coder or an entrepreneur. On top of everything, the assertion of an "art bias"— while art programs are systematically being eliminated from public education programs across the country by politicians (many of whom are making the exact same points as the academics)— strikes me as being a bit biased in its own way.

The author continued his subtle assault on the concept of art-as-ultimate-definition-of-creativity with the assertion that "Creativity isn't about freedom from concrete facts. Rather, fact-finding and deep research are vital stages in the creative process."

Maybe that's true if you are trying to invent a better mousetrap. But, it has nothing to do with finding your own creative expression.

The heart of the article addresses an idea that has become more prevalent over time: those things that cannot in some way be quantified, scientifically accounted for, or explained have no actual value and, therefore, no reason for being. And, as we live in a society where the perceived, quantifiable value of something has become its primary defining feature, this perspective renders ephemeral things (like art) as being utterly worthless.

One of the author's premises appears to be that creativity is basically a form of problem solving. Contrary to this, I would suggest that while problem solving may optimally be performed creatively, creativity doesn't optimally manifest itself through problem solving.

Additionally, Mr. Bronson clearly defined *creativity* in his article as the result of a highly refined intellectual process—down to the operational aspects of the brain when in a creative action. It was from this perspective that he and the scholars whose data he drew from were proposing to remedy the so-called creativity crisis by using memory games and other similar techniques that keep the mind limber and supple like a well-stretched muscle.

And that's where I disconnect from this article. As far as I'm concerned, the issue is highly subjective and depends thoroughly on whether you naturally use your right brain, your left brain, or a fluid interaction between both sides of your brain when you process incoming or outgoing data.

These definitions and explanations of the creative process forced me to examine my own relationship to creativity. I found myself recalling the state of my own consciousness while being creative. Had my experience of creativity been a series of conscious thoughts that developed from the need to solve a specific problem, and were then transformed to action? Was my experience of creativity a freeform series of events that occurred and were simultaneously executed from a completely unconscious place? Or, was it a wacky combination of the two?

Problem solving is an important element in record production, as nearly all recording projects have problems that require solutions.

And although being an artist is a creative endeavor, it certainly isn't always about solving specific problems by employing discreet, measurable, knowable parameters. When an architect creates a building, he is working within and responding to specific parameters. He is, in effect, solving a problem—albeit, creatively.

However, when an artist writes a piece of music or paints a picture, he isn't necessarily solving a problem. Unless the work in question was specifically commissioned, there is no explicable reason for an artist to create anything, apart from his need to express himself. This need—and not the goal to solve a specific problem—can be envisioned as the basis for the inception of all art.

Some occupations require a rationalized, left-brain form of creativity in order to enhance execution. A true artist creates because he is compelled to, out of necessity and often from an unconscious place. With this in mind, the concept of artistry itself creates somewhat of a pushback against the paradigm established in this article—that all creativity is something measurable and, thereby, can be understood and controlled.

I took stock of my own function as a record producer. Sometimes I am a problem solver, but often I am also an artist. In seeing this, I began to realize that although I have creatively solved problems from a conscious place, I have almost never created anything *artistically* from a conscious place.

It's only when I do prep work with an artist's music that I am even semiaware of what is happening. With song orchestrations or arrangements, I'll tend to run the part back and forth in my head until an answer comes—usually out of thin air. Once in a while I'll imagine orchestrating different instrument textures playing different parts until I come up with one that works best for the application.

When this happens, I feel as though I'm somewhere else, communing with a vast, incomprehensible intelligence that completely dwarfs and submerges my own.

I began to realize that anything I did consciously while in a creative process seemed to be more a function of my ego than a function of what I knew as "creativity." Many of the things I recalled doing were the very things over which I felt a sense of ownership; the types of things I could refer to in an interview and say, "Yes, that was my idea..."

In fact, giving the matter further consideration, I could scarcely recall *anything* I'd actually done while deeply absorbed in creative work—even when I mentally went fishing for instrument parts. I could sometimes recall the part, I just couldn't recall the process, or the mechanics I engaged to get the part. In fact, I felt like every idea had come from somewhere outside of me, as if unseen hands had hurled a ball at me from dark, stygian depths. It felt as if I'd done all the artistic stuff in a great big fog, but always instinctively knew where I was.

The recognition of this sense of "focused unawareness" made it clear to me that as an artist I often wasn't conscious, in a traditional sense, while in creative process. This led me to consider a mode of creativity that has nothing to do with any intellectual process and can't be harnessed or dominated by any human contrivance.

From my experience, the nonintellectual form of creativity seems to be something ephemeral and amorphous. It defies intellect and understanding, is impossible to quantify, and doesn't exist to yield a specific result in any endeavor. It simply *is*.

This other form of creativity manifests itself uniquely through each individual via whatever media or mode of expression that individual is drawn to. My experience is that it seems to have no general or specific point of origin in the conscious human mind and emanates instead from the subconscious. Therefore, it often can't be consciously generated at will, and very few individuals are able to engage their conscious creativity together with it.

In spite of its vague and elusive locality, I have found myself experiencing this state while in every variety of creative process and for as long as I can remember. If I were to describe my own somatic experience of it, I'd say that it sometimes feels like a warmth in the center of my body, sometimes a feeling of soaring through immense valleys, and sometimes it's a feeling of simply floating in space.

This is a contrast to much of the popular music I've encountered recently, which feels mechanical and increasingly devoid of substance, depth, and creative/expressive force—all form and no substance.

At its extremes, recent popular music evokes two discrete emotional states: (1) intense, unbridled rage (or intense pornographic sexuality, which is purely about sensory gratification and devoid of any feeling), and (2) an almost asexual, wispy state of inertia. In spite of their apparent opposite polarity, both of these states signify the same thing for their audiences—an all-encompassing state of numbness.

At the same time, there have been tremendous efforts made by contemporary musicians who are attempting to do something credible by emulating or openly copying musical styles of times gone by.

Why is it that a large segment of the newest generation of musicians have deified and shamelessly imitated old-guard artists from Led Zeppelin to Muddy Waters to Etta James roughly forty years after most of them peaked? Is it because no new artist has any original ideas and there's nothing worth recycling other than forty-year-old pop music? I don't recall any artists attempting in a similar manner to imitate Glenn Miller or doo-wop music when I was in my teens in the 1970s. Oops—forgot about Sha Na Na. They were kind of a niche act though, and not exactly ruling the charts.

It would be too easy to dismiss this phenomenon as a few isolated instances of erratic behavior from some sassy young folks who possess an encyclopedic knowledge of popular music. The only problem is, that conclusion doesn't make any sense. The world is full of imaginative, creative people—no less so than at any other period in history. What I'm talking about feels more like extreme desperation—as if there's a mass exodus taking place in which everyone is blindly groping around for something they can't perceive and don't understand but are absolutely starved for. Perhaps all the aforementioned imitating is some form of compensation for an elusive element that artists are missing in their medium—something they can't quite get a fix on but desperately need to connect with.

As it happens, the elusive element that these young artists are searching for isn't to be found in copying the form or structure of the work of earlier artists. In fact, what these young artists are searching is the same joyous, weightless sensation that arises from the ephemeral form of creativity.

The problem is that while many contemporary artists are able to experience this specific feeling from listening to older records, they are unable to generate it through their own work. Instead of going after what intrinsically makes that music so vital, they are appropriating the form of it over its substance. This is one reason that they try to emulate older records, sometimes integrating bits and pieces, sometimes incorporating elements en masse, down to the techniques of how they were recorded— even using the same types of recording equipment to do so.

As mentioned in previous chapters, these issues are compounded by the fact that my generation appears to have lost the fundamental ability or desire to gift or pay their knowledge forward to future generations. For some reason, the idea of philanthropy, mentoring, or doing anything simply for the sake of preserving and maintaining important information has been replaced by an overriding need to be compensated accordingly for one's time and effort. In fact, this seems to be part of a much larger societal issue that is corrupting and spoiling the humanity in people at every level.

Additionally, there is undue pressure on today's musicians to generate success well beyond their capabilities. This pressure is brought to bear by those captains of the music industry whose only concerns are their financial bottom lines and quarterly earnings reports. On top of this, there is an emphasis on entitlement and underperforming, which has gradually pervaded society over the past twenty-five years (and is described at length in *The Me Generation*, by Jean Twenge).

The existence of music and art in any society has always served a far greater role than a means to while away the hours while avoiding the realities of school, work, or life. Music is a subtle form of communication between humans, a deeper (and more universally recognizable) language than words, a pure and perfect means by which we can recognize others from our tribe. Music is a galvanizing societal force—the only true means of recognizing and speaking to divinity while existing in a largely secular culture that looks upon the unquantifiable as having no apparent meaning.

Unlike most other modes of expression, music is literally "felt" or experienced in a sensory manner. Its essence is something that can be analyzed, quantified, valued, or coopted by neither science nor commerce.

Sadly, this experience seems to be heading toward extinction as music becomes less viable as a vehicle of personal expression. I sometimes wonder if this potential extinction is nothing more than the flow of progress, a natural aspect of evolution as the landscape of artistic media goes digital. Or, is it an aberration, whose inevitability can be mitigated only through care and attention?

Whatever the case, I feel that those of us who have experience and passion for what we do need to recognize what is at stake. We need to take a stand, speak up, and provide viable alternatives to others who are anxious or compelled to find their place in the creative flow. By sharing our passion, we show others how to find and experience their passion. By sharing our knowledge and experience, we are able to gift a three-dimensional sensory impression of this experience to those who are receptive.

It has been said that knowledge is power. If this is true, too many artists in contemporary popular music are powerless. Although we as a society have such unprecedented access to information, much of it is confusing, confounding, or downright useless. One must work overtime to find the grains of knowledge that exist in the mountains of information to which we are constantly exposed.

Additionally, we are at a point where verifiable data has become virtually indistinguishable from advertising or sales pitches. This is clearly intentional on the part of advertisers, as presenting advertisements in the form of factual information is an ideal way to sell products. This makes it even more difficult for those who seek knowledge, but have no compass to guide them.

There is a time to teach by example and a time to use the DIY approach, but this very moment in time calls for an entirely different methodology. Unless the knowledge that is desperately needed can be shared and disseminated by individuals who possess it, all will be lost. This is a time for mentors who will selflessly transfer their own knowledge to those talented individuals who desire it. The Internet is an amazing resource, but it can't replace the visceral experience of assimilating knowledge directly from an individual with practical experience.

The creative process encompasses a great deal more than simply making things, problem solving, or being productive. It isn't merely another intellectual process that can be consciously understood or enhanced by learning a couple of brain-building memory exercises.

The author of the article "The Creativity Crisis" was doing a tremendous service, mainly by stating that creativity needs to be recognized. The focus on enhancing creativity is also important. However, it is imperative that both aspects of creativity are acknowledged and emphasized—not merely the intellectual aspect. Just as there are training exercises to improve mental power, elasticity, and capacity, there are also means to put a person deeper in touch with her own sense of personal expression, whatever that winds up being.

The expressive creative process offers us unique insight into ourselves, and as we see more of who we are, we will gradually have the same insight regarding other people. This can pertain to anyone from family members to random individuals we might encounter—all are genuinely unique, different from us, and special.

One defining characteristic of modern society is that we have gradually lost sight of one another. We have begun to perceive those around us less as individuals and more as extensions of ourselves. This is one reason that people behave toward one another with increasing callousness. It has become too easy to hide behind a computer screen, a wireless device, or the steering wheel of a car instead of relating to and interacting with other people.

There is something remarkable about simply being alive, being sentient. In being sentient, we have the experience of interacting with other people in every moment and seeing how—instead of being extensions of one another—we very much resemble and reflect one another.

29

THE THREE FORMS OF CREATIVITY

Over time, I have encountered three discreet forms of creativity in nearly all actions or activities. The first two pertain to the endeavors of people; the third pertains to creativity on the grandest scale possible, and in every imaginable realm. These three forms of creativity are:

1. **Linear, reactive, occupational, ideated, or outcome-based creativity.** This is creativity that arises in response to a conscious need (reactive), involves engaging a conscious thought process (or series of thought processes or ideas) and, ideally, results in a predictable outcome. It is linear or outcome based because all possible results derived from incorporating this approach can fall only within a specific range or guideline, because the idea or thought process is always being applied to something known: a known problem that requires a solution. This outcome is dictated by the awareness, knowledge, or intellect of the individual performing the creative act. Linear creativity can occur only by incorporating predetermined parameters. Linear creativity is the result of an intellectual process, and is consciously applied to mental endeavors, such as problem solving.

2. **Nonlinear, expressive creativity.** This form of creativity is pure essence, formless form, and emanates directly

from the unconscious. It is nonlinear because it operates in accordance with no apparent timetable and manifests itself concretely only as a peripheral aspect of and relative to an individual's ability in his specific discipline or his ability to be a good receiver or channel. This capability to receive information from the unconscious is directly proportional to individual sensitivity and hypersensitivity. Nonlinear creativity is not relative to anything in a person's existence; it is merely a natural process in humans. It is ephemeral and, as such, directs its host instead of being consciously applied.

3. **Spontaneous, universal creativity.** This form of creativity is an expression of everything within and around us on a moment-to-moment basis. It is present in the generative aspects of all beings and worlds and is manifested in breathing, speaking, being conceived, being born, cataclysms, earthquakes, stars going supernova, and so on. Our engagement with this form of creativity is unavoidable, as it is present in our autonomous bodily functions, everything we do, say, express, and act. It is the form of creativity from which all others are derived and, therefore, encapsulates them. It is creativity and being in its purest and most elemental form.

In nonlinear creativity, the feeling comes before the idea. In linear creativity, the idea comes before the feeling. Under ideal conditions, these two forms of creativity will interact. This is how the most brilliant composers and artists are able to make works for hire on command.

30

AN IDEA IS A START POINT, NOT AN END POINT

Having a creative idea is like being handed a blessing from heaven.

Often, people find themselves foundering and grasping at straws all the way through their creative process simply because they are wracking their brains to come up with one good idea. While they wait for a flash of brilliance, they'll go on a series of mental fishing expeditions, trying all sorts of things to pick up their slack—most of which wind up leading nowhere.

And then, suddenly from out of the blue, it comes. This idea could be anything: a melody, a unique way of recording an instrument, an unusual sound, or an overall approach to a body of work that makes up a recording.

When you are touched by such a timely and necessary insight, your entire world is instantaneously upended. You have been whacked by divine inspiration and are the recipient of a message just for you sent from an intelligence far greater than anything we mere mortals can comprehend.

And then, once you've received this message, you go back and attempt to plug it into the framework of whatever you've been working on so diligently. You give it great credence, you basically allow this idea to redefine and reframe everything else you've been working on.

After all, this is a brand-new, fresh idea that came directly to you from the cosmos itself. Because of this, this new idea is peerless, priceless, and unquestionable, and must therefore be heeded without any doubt.

Many of us have been in this position on numerous occasions. We were doggedly searching for a way into something or other we were working on and then, voila! The answer cometh.

Generally, this is how creative dilemmas get solved: You wait for a solution. It suddenly arrives without any rational thought (or even a heads-up) and is then made concrete through the machinations of rational thought. It comes into this world from the ether, from the other side.

When your wish comes true, you sometimes wind up with an idea that fits perfectly with the structures you've been building on and the process of incorporating it is completely fluid. Sometimes, you wind up with an idea that, while absolutely brilliant, doesn't quite fit with everything else you've been working on.

When the latter instance occurs, somewhere in the conversion process—from those etheric realms to abstract feeling to concrete thought—your ego sneakily insinuates itself into the picture. With the appearance of the ego, this idea you've been gifted suddenly takes on an entirely new meaning relative to your work and your creative process. Suddenly, the idea that appeared to be so inspiring and so compelling becomes a millstone, an albatross around your neck. It begins to strangle you and to drag you down.

This is because you have been languishing under the mistaken belief that you must use this idea *exactly* as it came to you, one way or another. It must be incorporated into your work and your process even if it doesn't jibe well with preexisting ideas and structures that you have been laboring over. You feel obligated to use this idea, even if you wind up having to junk the large pieces of work you've already begun to flesh out and develop.

That's right about when things start to fall apart. You're stuck jamming a square peg into a round hole. You begin to feel as if nothing's right and you're going nuts. And why are you experiencing this intense reaction? In part, because your ego is convinced that since it detected and transcribed this amazing idea from out of the ether, your ego must have actually come up with it. And because of this, you're ready to destroy everything that was previously so good only because you need to somehow incorporate this new idea.

One more reason is that this idea is new, and in the context of old familiar structures, anything new must be better.

Predictably, the next stage of this process is when, after banging your head against the wall to get things to fit (and, in so-doing, turning your project into a game of Jenga), the shiny new idea begins to peter out and become stale. One reason for this is, in the ensuing drama, you have missed the true significance of this idea and why it came your way. Another reason is that in the process of forcing this new idea to work with your existing structures, you have made it more important than anything else and are literally working it to death. Being a great artist is not just about listening to what comes to you from the outside, but also being a great interpreter of this information. Sometimes an idea is merely a bridge—a means of progressing to yet another idea or a series of other ideas. Ideas aren't always meant to be taken literally or used as you get them. Sometimes they come from a voice within that is constantly whispering nothing more than "Listen, listen . . . ," only so you can be more in tune with your feelings.

Ephemeral creative flow is far different from linear creativity. In linear creativity, an idea is generated as a means of solving a specific problem. Therefore, from the linear perspective, an idea is an ego-generated contrivance that is converted into a quantifiable end result when it is brought into concrete form.

However, in ephemeral creativity, an idea is nothing more than a signpost or the starting point of a new adventure. The relative time line is less important, or, as the saying goes, the main thrill is in getting there. In other words, the process of receiving an idea from a nonlinear perspective isn't born from the need to solve a problem, and the idea doesn't necessarily have to remain intact once it has been received.

In ephemeral creativity, an idea is exactly what it's meant to be, but is often not what it appears to be. Sometimes, an idea is a marker on a creative adventure already in progress. Sometimes it's the beginning to a completely unknown and unexpected path. Sometimes it's the end to a familiar way of doing things, and sometimes it's the start of an avalanche of new ideas.

And sometimes an idea is a test—a way of reminding us to be fluid, to be open and flexible. In ephemeral creativity, an idea can be completely subjective and its significance known only to the artist who then sees it through to fruition or oblivion.

In ephemeral creativity, one thing an idea *never* is, is something that is meant to be engraved in stone or to become a law that is strictly followed to the absolute letter. It is never a be-all or an end-all in or of itself. The text of an idea—what it appears to be telling us—isn't always the actual significance of the idea or how it will ultimately end up.

So, how do you discover what a specific idea signifies or means to you? Start by dissecting it. Ask yourself: what can this possibly mean to me? Put it into context with dreams you've had, odd flights of fancy, what you ate for dinner last week. Consider it figuratively and don't rush to understand it literally. Study this idea, listen to what it is really telling you, and then follow its directives as you've reframed and recontextualized them.

Then go where it directs you without fear and without worrying that it may lead you down a blind alley in your creative process.

Allow it to filter and matriculate into your prior work gradually, with ease and without force.

Permit everything to interact and to gel.

You may choose to follow each idea through to its logical conclusion, or simply to the next idea it brings you to. You are also open to turning on a dime and completely jettisoning the idea if it begins to rub against you in any way that feels increasingly wrong. This awareness helps you to be constantly mindful, in the moment, and completely spontaneous—perpetually tapped into the source of complete artistic freedom and bliss.

31

OBJECTIVITY, INCENTIVE, AND OWNERSHIP

Maintaining objectivity on a recording project may be the most difficult task a record producer can have. It's a bit like trying to watch your own mind think—at the same time, it is something you must constantly be aware of.

At some stage in the process, most record producers will develop a proprietary attitude toward the project they are working on. It doesn't matter if the producer isn't the artist, isn't performing on the recording, and hasn't written or arranged a single note of music. The producer has still contributed some creative input to the recording and, when she does this, she has already begun developing a sense of ownership toward it.

There are upsides and downsides to this situation. Conventional wisdom tells us that people tend to work harder on things they either are personally invested in or have a financial interest in. When one becomes invested in any undertaking, it isn't always because they love what they are working on. Often, they have been incentivized to work hard by the promise of a big payoff at the project's end.

Frankly, it's pretty hard not to experience proprietary feelings about a recording, even if you are the sort of producer who is completely detached from the creative process. I've experienced it frequently and seen other people do the same thing.

Some time ago, I coproduced a short project for a well-known publishing company. There was no budget involved, and we had two weeks to work on four songs that (as is often the case) quickly became five songs.

The entire project was done soup to nuts within the two weeks allotted. The finished master was sent off to a few labels for consideration and—wonder of wonders—the publisher got a bite from a major. In spite of all this, somewhere along the way one of the artists in the band had a major freak-out and suddenly decided he hated everything we'd done, fled his hipster conclave of Silverlake and moved to Kansas—tie-dyed shirts and all.

Having recognized this person's self-destructive nature, I had honestly seen this coming, but my coproducer was blindsided and took it rather hard. In fact, for the next few years, whenever we'd get together, somewhere in our conversation, he'd bring up this ill-fated project and what an ass the artist who moved to Kansas had been. My colleague had put a lot of effort into the project, and clearly felt robbed of a potential slam-dunk.

However, he had conveniently ignored the fact that throughout the two weeks we worked on this project, the artist who freaked out had been sending consistent signals that this implosion was an impending possibility. The guy would show up at the studio and constantly rag on how bad everything sounded, how the music felt forced, how uncomfortable he was with his performances—even while everyone else was raving about how good it all was.

This artist was in a constantly fragile emotional state, and having something actually work out for him wasn't amenable with his worldview. Meanwhile, my colleague had wanted this project to succeed so desperately that he fooled himself into believing he had the power to somehow avert the inevitable.

A very long time ago (around the time the Magna Carta was signed) I worked on a different recording and I decided to pull out all the stops, sonically. I had an engineer modify a multi-track tape machine to make everything I recorded sound deeper, punchier, and heavier. I also made a fantastically profligate investment in additional recording equipment to facilitate my vision for this project, which I saw as being the paramount artistic statement of my lifetime. After all, you only live once.

This project met all my expectations. It sounded amazing. At one point, I recall a studio manager walking into the control room—it was his studio where we were working—and shaking his head in wonder, announcing that this was the best recording of drums he'd ever heard. And he was listening to a slave reel that had been bounced from the master.

Holy crap. Every day, I was on top of the world. The record was thunderous, magnificent—I was going to be a hero and change the face of recorded music. Then, the recording was over and the record company hired a mix engineer—who prophetically stated when we met, "I've come to wreck your mix…er, mix your record." He was as good as his word, and without further ado, very ably proceeded to wreck my mix. I went from the heights of triumph to the depths of utter devastation inside of a month. All my well-laid plans were dashed to bits. My masterpiece metamorphosed effortlessly into a crappy, substandard metal record. All the high concept and sonic grandeur I'd created to conceal the mediocrity of the material was stripped away. This turd couldn't be polished, especially when the varnish had been stripped off it.

I had owned this record in my mind for so long, it had ceased to occur to me that it wasn't my property. My perspective was skewed and my objectivity had run well aground. In the aftermath, I was inconsolably miserable for a full year afterward. I kept replaying the entire project back in my head, and blaming myself for everything that went wrong.

One night, I was in a car with someone when a song from the record came on the radio. This guy made an awful face and said loudly, "Now that's just the kind of crappy substandard metal record I can't stand." That pronouncement somehow put things into perspective for me and I could finally move on.

A sense of ownership is reasonable from the person who writes or performs a piece of music. It is also reasonable from the person who produces the recording, as she becomes deeply involved on various levels. However, this feeling of propriety does not always benefit the project or anyone on it.

No matter what motivates a producer's proprietary feelings toward a project she is producing, unless she is conscious of these feelings and understands what is motivating them, they can potentially compromise her objectivity and her ability to do her job.

The coproducer from my first story has a real talent for selecting people to produce, but also openly acknowledges that he has a blind spot when it comes to objectively analyzing his artists' work *after* he starts producing them. Because of this, he constantly finds himself making excuses for their shortcomings and ignoring their warning signs. Having experienced this same issue on other projects, I must often taken a step back in order to examine my own motives when I'm feeling more proprietary in my work—acting out my need for dominance and simultaneously experiencing a loss of objectivity. With this in mind, I try to reexamine what I am working on after recontextualizing it through the lens of this understanding.

Examining your intent with extreme prejudice is vitally important because it provides you with a consistent barometer regarding how and why you are motivated to act from moment to moment. Admittedly, it can be difficult to assess yourself in this way. However, the job you have chosen is also difficult. If you decide to enter this work casually and without consideration, your involvement in it will be largely casual and unconscious. For this reason alone, considering your motivation is very important.

So far, we have established that there are positive and negative connotations to having proprietary feelings toward a record production. We have also established that a record producer is best when he can be as objective as possible regarding his work, and that a proprietary feeling toward this work often corrupts his ability to be objective. Generally speaking, before he has heard an artist's material (unless he is already familiar with the artist's prior work and has some kind of expectation about it) a producer generally has no idea about what it sounds like, and therefore, no preconceptions about it. But once he has listened to this music for the first time, he has already lost some of his objectivity, the way a new car loses a portion of its value the moment it's purchased and driven off the lot. If he is absolutely committed to the project, he begins to identify himself with it, thereby becoming invested in it, and develops a proprietary attitude toward it.

So, how does a record producer reestablish his objectivity on a project when he has already begun to lose his perspective?

At its essence, being critically objective goes straight back to the first instant a producer hears a piece of music she will be working on and has that intuitive feeling about whether she loves or hates it. In that moment, the producer is not a producer, she is not a creative person or an artist; she is simply a listener like any other—nothing more than an ordinary person who is moved by the power of music.

At this moment, she is at the height of her objectivity because her feelings are untainted by preconceptions or agenda. She is free to judge what she hears honestly and based solely upon what she feels from it. Her reactions to what she hears are completely connected to her unconscious mind. She essentially has no choice to do otherwise.

Once this moment of absolute objectivity has passed, she starts incorporating her own needs, ego, and motivations into the mix, all of which consequently affect her viewpoint, her ability to be critically objective, and ultimately, her usefulness. She may feel passionately about this piece of music or hear great potential in it that inspires her. In this case, she becomes incentivized by passion—it motivates her and stimulates her creative process. Some of the greatest art in history has emanated from this energy.

Imagine for a moment that you're listening to a piece of music that you may be producing and it's surprisingly good. You hear promise in it. The artist is very talented. There are great, ear-catching moments, but there are also flaws and inconsistencies. You see the potential, but you know it can be better.

You listen to this piece of music a few more times and you suddenly become aware that it has pervaded your thoughts. You even start humming it when you're not thinking about anything in particular. Suddenly, all the imperfections in the song have vanished and all you can see is unmitigated perfection. You forget all the issues you initially saw and can't imagine how it could be made better.

In some ways, this is similar to falling in love. When you first meet someone, you can clearly see who she is, but as your relationship gradually changes and you begin to develop feelings for her, the initial objectivity or impressions you have of her tend to vanish and are replaced by emotions (and hormones). As time goes by, these feelings mature and change into something completely different and it is virtually impossible to imagine this person the same way you did when you initially met her.

This is mitigated by the fact that people change and they are further recontextualized inside a relationship. A piece of music can also be altered but, just like a person, it retains its essential meaning and makeup no matter what is done to it. A mediocre or good song can be made better, but it will never be great. Its presentation can be altered, but its basic meaning cannot.

Take this piece of music you are so excited about. What is motivating you to be so excited about it? Is it something about the music that makes you love it, or is it something about you? Is it something you feel passionately about, is it something you feel will benefit you in some way, or are you just happy to have something to be working on?

Think back to when you first heard this piece of music. What was the first impression you had the moment you heard it? Does this recollection jibe with how you feel about this piece of music at this exact moment in time? If it doesn't, what has changed? If you felt there were aspects of this music that could be better when you first heard it, what were they and do you still feel the same way?

Now, de-incentivize and divest yourself from the process entirely. Imagine that instead of producing this piece of music you are going to facilitate it, and when you are done, you will be handing it off, either to the band and an engineer who will be recording it, or to another producer. In this case, your job is done the moment the artist takes his music to be recorded. As a result, you have absolutely no ownership whatsoever regarding anything. Whether the music succeeds or fails will be based on how good it is, not on how good you think it is or want it to be because it may put some money into your bank account. Your compensation for working on this is guaranteed whether it makes money or not. You can be as critical and as forensic with it as you wish.

Now, go back to this piece of music and listen to it again. Stop winding yourself up about how much potential it has, how record companies have been climbing all over one another to sign this artist, how it's the type of music that everyone is listening to on the radio this month, how great the bridge melody is, how cool the drumbeat is in the second verse, or how good the recording sounds. Listen for all the flaws, all the ugliness and beauty, all the places where you feel like the music loses you, and all the places where it lifts you up and carries you effortlessly along.

More important than anything else, listen only with your intuition and consider this question: *how does this piece of music make you feel right now?*

ABRIDGED DISCOGRAPHY

ALBUMS

Temporary Music 1, Material (Celluloid, 1979)

Temporary Music 2, Material (Celluloid, 1980)

"It's a Holiday," Material, featuring Nona Hendryx (from *ZE Christmas Compilation*, Ze Records, 1981)

Memory Serves, Material (Elektra/Musician, 1981)

"Lizard Point," Brian Eno (from *Ambient 4: On Land*, Caroline, 1982)

One Down, Material (Elektra/Asylum Records"?>> 1982)

Nona, Nona Hendryx (RCA Records, 1982)

The Art of Defense, Nona Hendryx (RCA Records, 1983)

Future Shock, Herbie Hancock (Sony Records, 1983)

At the Feet of the Moon, The Parachute Club (RCA Records, 1984)

Love's Imperfection, Idle Eyes (Warner Bros., Canada, 1986)

The Uplift Mofo Party Plan, Red Hot Chili Peppers (EMI/Capitol Records, 1987)

Mother's Milk, Red Hot Chili Peppers (EMI/Capitol Records, 1989)

Mercurotones, The Buck Pets (Island Records, 1990)

Why Do Birds Sing?, The Violent Femmes (Warner Bros., 1990)

Grave Dancers Union, Soul Asylum (Sony Records, 1992)

Superunknown, Soundgarden (A&M Records, 1994)

Ozzmosis, Ozzy Osbourne (Epic Records, 1995)

White Light, White Heat, White Trash, Social Distortion (Epic Records, 1996)

Big Windshield, Little Mirror, Foam (Epic Records, 1997)

Sense and Sensuality, Nicky Holland (Epic Records, 1997)

Celebrity Skin, Hole (Geffen Records, 1998)

Mechanical Animals, Marilyn Manson (Nothing/Interscope, 1998)

The Verve Pipe, The Verve Pipe (RCA Records, 1999)

Untouchables, Korn (Sony Records, 2002)

Natural Selection, Fuel (Epic Records, 2003)

Nightcrawler, Pete Yorn (Sony Records, 2004)

And the Glass Handed Kites, Mew (Sony Records, 2005)

The Bronx, The Bronx (Island/Def Jam, 2006)

A Public Display of Affection, The Blizzards (Universal Music Ireland, 2006)

Nobody's Daughter, Hole (Mercury Records, 2010)

The Domino Effect, The Blizzards (Universal Music Ireland, 2011)

Plus/Minus, Mew (Sony Records, 2015)

SINGLES

"Discourse"/"Slow Murder," Material (Red, 1980)

"Bustin' Out"/"Over and Over," Material, featuring Nona Hendryx (Ze Records, 1981)

"Ciguri"/"Detached," Material (Celluloid, 1981)

"Change the Beat," Fab Five Freddy (Celluloid, 1982)

"Grandmixer Cuts It Up," Grandmixer DST (Celluloid, 1982)

"I'm the One," Material, featuring Bernard Fowler (Elektra, 1982)

"Keep It Confidential," Nona Hendryx (RCA, 1982)

"Memories," Material, featuring Whitney Houston and Archie Shepp (Elektra, 1982)

"The Roxy," Phase II (Celluloid, 1982)

"Autodrive," Herbie Hancock (Sony Records, 1983)

"Crazy Cuts," Grandmixer DST (Island, 1983)

"For a Few Dollars More," Material (Celluloid, 1983)

"I Sweat," Nona Hendryx, featuring Afrika Bambaataa (RCA Records, 1983)

"Rockit," Herbie Hancock (Sony Records, 1983)

"Strong Me Strong"/"Disco Reggae," Yellowman (Sony Records, 1983)

"At the Feet of the Moon," The Parachute Club (RCA Records, 1984)

"Sexual Intelligence," The Parachute Club (RCA Records, 1984)

"Black on Black"/"Baby Doll," Lisa Dalbello (Capitol Records, 1985)

"Love's Imperfection," Idle Eyes (Warner Bros., 1985)

"Behind the Sun," The Red Hot Chili Peppers (EMI/Capitol Records, 1987)

"Fight Like a Brave," The Red Hot Chili Peppers (from The Uplift Mofo Party Plan, EMI/Capitol Records, 1987)

"Me and My Friends," The Red Hot Chili Peppers, track was not released as a single but received radio airplay (from *The Uplift Mofo Party Plan*, EMI/Capitol Records, 1987)

"Higher Ground," The Red Hot Chili Peppers (EMI America, 1989)

"Knock Me Down," The Red Hot Chili Peppers (EMI/Capitol Records, 1989)

"Taste the Pain," The Red Hot Chili Peppers (EMI, 1989)

"Do You Really Want to Hurt Me?" The Violent Femmes (Warner Bros., 1990)

"Pearls," The Buck Pets (Island Records, 1990)

"Black Gold," Soul Asylum (Sony Records, 1992)

"Runaway Train," Soul Asylum (Sony Records, 1992)

"Somebody to Shove," Soul Asylum (Sony Records, 1992)

"Black Hole Sun," Soundgarden (A&M Records, 1993)

"The Day I Tried to Live," Soundgarden (A&M Records, 1993)

"Fell on Black Days," Soundgarden (A&M Records, 1993)

"Spoonman," Soundgarden (A&M Records, 1993)

"Blind Man"/"Walk on the Water," Aerosmith (Geffen Records, 1994)

"I Just Want You," Ozzy Osbourne (Epic Records, 1995)

"Perry Mason" Ozzy Osbourne (Epic Records, 1995)

"See You on the Other Side," Ozzy Osbourne (Epic Records, 1995)

"Sunshine of Your Love," Living Color (Epic Records, 1995)

"Don't Drag Me Down," Social Distortion (Epic Records, 1996)

"I Was Wrong," Social Distortion (Epic Records, 1996)

"Awful," Hole (Geffen Records, 1998)

"Celebrity Skin," Hole (Geffen Records, 1998)

"Coma White," Marilyn Manson (Nothing/Interscope, 1998)

"I Don't Like the Drugs (But the Drugs Like Me)," Marilyn Manson (Nothing/Interscope, 1998)

"The Dope Show," Marilyn Manson (Nothing/Interscope, 1998)

"Malibu," Hole (Geffen Records, 1998)

"Rock Is Dead," Marilyn Manson (Nothing/Interscope, 1998)

"Hero," The Verve Pipe (RCA Records, 1999)

"Alone, I Break," Korn (Epic Records, 2002)

"Here to Stay," Korn (Epic Records, 2002)

"Thoughtless," Korn (Epic Records, 2002)

"Falls on Me," Fuel (Epic Records, 2004)

"Apocalypso," Mew (Sony Records, 2005)

"Special," Mew (Sony Records, 2005)

"Why Are You Looking Grave," Mew (Sony Records, 2005)

"The Zookeeper's Boy," Mew (Sony Records, 2005)

"History's Stranglers," The Bronx (Island/Def Jam, 2006)

"Shitty Future," The Bronx (Island/Def Jam, 2006)

"White Guilt," The Bronx (Island/Def Jam, 2006)

"Miss Fantasia Preaches," The Blizzards (Universal, 2006)

"Fantasy," The Blizzards (Universal, 2007)

"Postcards," The Blizzards (Universal, 2008)

"Trust Me, I'm a Doctor," The Blizzards (Universal, 2008)

"Buy It, Sell It," The Blizzards (Universal, 2009)

"Pacific Coast Highway," Hole (Mercury Records, 2010)

"Skinny Little Bitch," Hole (Mercury Records, 2010)

"Wedding Day," Courtney Love (Cherry Forever, 2014)

"You Know My Name," Courtney Love (Cherry Forever, 2014)

"Satellites," Mew (Sony Records, 2015)

"Waterslides," Mew (Sony Records, 2015)